PARALYZED

TO

POWERFUL

LESSONS FROM A
QUADRIPLEGIC'S JOURNEY

ROBERT PAYLOR
AND JASON COLE

Published in Roseville, CA.

For more information, visit the author's website at www.robertpaylor.com.

Library of Congress Control Number: 2025905415

Hardcover ISBN: 979-8-9927793-2-5
Paperback ISBN: 979-8-9927793-0-1
E-book ISBN: 979-8-9927793-1-8
Audiobook ISBN: 979-8-9927793-3-2

Printed in the United States of America

DEDICATION

To Mom, Dad, and Brant

I couldn't have asked for a better family. You have been there for me through every moment and have helped me build a life beyond anything I could have dreamed. I love you all beyond words.

To Karsen

You are the answer to my prayers and the most incredible person I have ever met. I don't know where I'd be without you. Our marriage is the greatest gift I have ever received, and it's the blessing of my life to vow my heart and love to you.

To Coach Clark and Coach Billups

None of my accomplishments over the last eight years would have been possible without you. Most of all, you helped me find my purpose. I'm forever grateful for your coaching and support.

TABLE OF CONTENTS

INTRODUCTION

WHAT PARALYZES YOU?
Whether we recognize it or not, we are all paralyzed by something. Each of us has experienced it at one point or another—the feeling of being powerless, unable to move forward. There's the mental paralysis that grips us when we face overwhelming challenges and the emotional paralysis that leaves us feeling helpless or unfulfilled.

What paralyzes me is obvious. I have spent every day of the last eight years in a wheelchair, and by definition, I am a quadriplegic. It's a condition that has changed my life and added complexity to almost every daily task, from getting dressed to brushing my teeth, taking a shower, and nearly everything in between. Just by looking at me, you can see that I go through a lot each day.

The wheelchair I move through life in, the scar on my neck, and the atrophy in my muscles are all visible reminders of my paralysis. But most of my battles, nobody can see on the surface, and I'm sure you can relate.

Think of the self-doubt that whispers, "You're not good enough," the fear that halts you before you begin, or the anxiety that grips you in social situations. These are the silent adversaries that wage war within, the ones that no amount of physical therapy can cure. And yet, they are just as real, just as crippling as any physical paralysis.

Take, for instance, the high school student who dreams of attending college but is paralyzed by the fear of

1

rejection. Or the aspiring entrepreneur who wants to start their own business but is held back by the fear of failure. Or the parent who struggles to make ends meet and feels paralyzed by the weight of their responsibilities. These are just a few examples of the many ways paralysis can affect our lives.

In eight years of battling paralysis, I've grown into a stronger person. I've learned how to be resilient in the face of adversity and maintain gratitude in the midst of hardship. While my injury took many of my physical abilities away, the fight to regain what I've lost fortified my mindset and instilled principles within me that I am confident have prepared me for any challenge I will face going forward.

It's not a stretch to say that I've gained far more than I lost through this injury, but that doesn't mean I recommend someone endure the same trials as I did to emerge stronger on the other side. Fortunately for you, you don't have to. What you need is empathy, the ability to see beyond yourself and connect with the struggles of others.

This book is the culmination of what I've learned to overcome any form of mental or emotional paralysis. I recount my journey of battling quadriplegia, taking you through my greatest triumphs and tragedies. While the experiences themselves are meant to inspire, each chapter contains a tool that has helped me through the greatest challenge of my life, the story of how I discovered it, and how I recommend you use it today. You can access the full strength of these tools if you approach this book with an outward-looking mindset and a willingness to apply these lessons to your own life.

To help you do that, I've included reflection questions at the end of each chapter. These are designed to prompt meaningful self-reflection and guide you in uncovering how the lessons in this book apply to your unique journey. I encourage you to take time to answer these questions honestly and thoughtfully, either by journaling, discussing them with a friend, or spending time in private contemplation.

But this book isn't a miracle cure. There are no mere words I can share that will make your challenges go away. I provide proven lessons that have helped me, but using them is up to you.

This also isn't a one-time fix. You will face challenges that threaten to paralyze you in some way every day, multiple times a day, for the rest of your life. The responsibility to step up to that adversity is on you.

While the path may be difficult and full of challenges, it's also rich with opportunities for growth and self-discovery. While paralysis may rob us of our abilities, it also holds the key to our liberation. It's only when we confront our innermost hardships that we begin to release their grip on our lives and forge a path toward empowerment.

So, as you prepare to read this book, think about what paralyzes you. Don't look on the surface; take the time to dive deep within yourself. What lies at the core of what holds you back?

Whatever it is, know you're not alone. We all have our battles to fight. But with the right mindset and the right tools, we can overcome any obstacle and emerge stronger, wiser, and more powerful than we ever thought possible.

Chapter 1

CONTROL YOUR MINDSET

Everything can be taken from a man but one thing: the last
of the human freedoms—to choose one's attitude in any
given set of circumstances, to choose one's own way.

—Viktor Frankl, *Man's Search for Meaning*

O N THE DAY I became a national champion, I also
prepared to die.

On May 6, 2017, I was twenty years old, lying
motionless in a hospital bed. I had been paralyzed after
two vertebrae and a disc in my neck had broken earlier
that day during the collegiate rugby national title game
against Arkansas State. I was a starter for the University
of California, Berkeley, the most dominant program in US
collegiate rugby history.

We had won the game, cementing my place alongside the
many players who had competed on the more than thirty
championship teams Cal produced. But at this moment, I
needed to draw on my rugby training to survive.

I had just received a grim report from a doctor at Santa
Clara Valley Medical Center. The doctor wasn't exactly
cold, but he was direct as he laid out the worst-case sce-
nario. I'm a practitioner of upbeat thinking, but there was

nothing upbeat about this moment and no amount of bedside manner was going to change that.

The doctor said I was probably never going to walk again, nor would I ever be able to move my hands. If I were lucky, I might one day be able to feed myself, like picking up a piece of pizza. He confirmed every worst fear I had been struggling with for the past several hours.

I was a prisoner of my body, likely a quadriplegic for life. The terror of having almost zero control of my movement was augmented by a bizarre sense of disorientation. I felt like a head attached to a body I could no longer feel or control.

Like an evil infomercial from a twisted universe, there was more. The doctor said I needed to have surgery almost immediately if I wanted any chance of even a moderate recovery. Not just any surgery, but high-risk surgery during which I could die.

Given my injury, I couldn't simply be turned over and operated on from the back of my neck. He had to operate on two of my lower cervical vertebrae and the disc in between—the C5 and C6 for those interested in the alphanumeric system of the spine—by entering from the front, moving my esophagus to the side, and working around the structure of my body. It was like trying to fix the axle of a car by going through the hood and around the engine.

I realize that's a jarring image for some people to imagine. Imagine how jarring it was to live through.

That news came on top of the pain, terror, and anxiety I already felt. In the hours since I had been hurt, that trio of factors had overtaken my body, spiking my temperature to a steady 103 degrees, with a brief peak at 105.

At one point during the examination process, I had to lie in an MRI scanner for nearly two and a half hours.

With my six-foot-five, 240-pound frame, I was a tight fit. My shoulders squeezed and my nose was only inches from the inner wall of the tubular machine. My anxiety surged as I struggled to keep my head perfectly still, feeling like I was trapped in a coffin.

The doctor gave me one hour to decide whether I would have the surgery, but the decision had already been made in my mind. I knew that in my heart as soon as he said it. There were no alternatives. There was no unwinding the events of earlier in the day. There was no looking back.

Or, as I had been trained about mental toughness by the great rugby coaches Jack Clark and Tom Billups at Cal: You have to focus on the next most important thing. Mistakes and setbacks are going to happen. Mental toughness is the ability not to let those mishaps get the best of you.

Life can set you off course in plenty of ways, from losing your job to facing illness or experiencing a relationship breakdown. In a rugby game, dwelling on a dropped pass or a blown tackle doesn't solve anything, and it might distract you from your next play. Focusing on your response is how you move forward.

The difference now was that the situation had become grave. I was playing a game where the stakes were my life. It was one thing to forget a mistake on the field and move on to the next play.

It was quite another challenge to focus on the next most important thing when I was playing for keeps. The clock was ticking, and I needed to get my affairs in order. This took every bit of my determination to extinguish the thoughts that threatened my focus. The adrenaline-soaked anxiety wasn't just sending my body temperature soaring; it was playing tricks on my mind.

I toggled between hoping I would wake up from this nightmare and facing the darkness of a confined future, if I were fortunate enough to survive surgery. Sometimes I questioned how this could possibly be God's plan for me.

I always believed that God had a plan for me and that His plan was good. I submitted my trust to Him, but I was terrified beyond explanation. I thought I was called to serve others. How could I help others when I couldn't even help myself? If God did have a plan for me, it seemed messed up.

I pictured myself sitting in a wheelchair in front of a window each day for the rest of my life, waiting for my mom to spoon-feed me. I wondered who would care for me when she passed away. I saw no love in my future. What woman could love the broken body now tethered to my head?

Decades of my future played out in seconds in my mind.

I fought those thoughts as I tried to focus on the task at hand. I told myself to get my head back in the game. What was next? What did I need to concentrate on? With one hour counting down, there was no time to spare.

I'm Catholic, so the first phone call I made was to my spiritual director. I asked him to send a priest to give me the Sacrament of Anointing of the Sick. That way if I died, my soul would be cleansed for heaven, and if I lived, I would have the gift of peace and courage to deal with the challenges that awaited me ahead. In that frantic moment, he shared the most profound advice I've ever received.

"Robert, what has happened to you is terrible, and throughout this journey there are going to be a lot of things you can't control," he said. "But the one thing you have control over is your mindset. Your optimism, your resilience, and your willingness to take on this challenge every day and fight are up to you. This injury can't take that away from you."

Challenges are guaranteed in life, and we can't control that, but we can always control how we respond. Success isn't determined by the circumstances we face. Success lies in our constructive response to those circumstances, regardless of how difficult they may be. That's the essence of controlling one's mindset, and that's a decision we always have command over.

That wisdom empowered me in a moment when I felt utterly powerless. Every reason to panic was staring me in the face, but my spiritual director's advice reminded me that my circumstances didn't control my mindset. I did. I steadied myself, holding tight to my composure as I navigated these terrifying moments.

I wanted to call and text my closest friends. Because I couldn't raise my arms more than a few inches and had no control of my fingers, my brother had to be my phone surrogate. He dialed each number, holding the phone in front of me while I made one FaceTime call after another.

My brother, Brant, was seventeen at the time, and he did way more than handle the phone. He handled his own emotions to help me keep mine together. He hadn't seen me get hurt that day because he was back home taking the SAT. My grandparents picked him up and drove him to Santa Clara.

We had an extremely close family, especially the relationship between my brother and me. We grew up in a semirural part of the Sacramento area called El Dorado Hills. Our house wasn't in a classic neighborhood with closely placed homes, and there weren't many other kids. Brant and I were not just brothers, we were best friends. We did *everything* together. I coached him at home and taught him everything I knew. I tried to be a role model for him and be strong for him.

As much as I wanted to see him before my surgery, I dreaded it as well. I knew seeing him could rip my heart out. I was weak and broken at that moment, and I didn't have any strength to show. I knew I wouldn't be able to handle him breaking down in front of me.

I couldn't be strong for him. I needed him to be strong for me, and I told my mom to tell him that before he came into the room. I told her he was not allowed to cry or show fear because if he did, it would shatter me.

When he came in, I couldn't look at him. I spoke to him in a choked-up voice, but I couldn't bring myself to look him in the eye. I could give him a quick glance, but that was all. I knew I wouldn't be able to speak if I looked at him. My emotions would have completely overcome me.

Here I was at the lowest point of my life. I could barely get the words out to tell him I loved him and that I would always love him. I don't remember him speaking a lot, and it's not something we've talked about in the years since, but he was the strongest person in the room that day when he held my phone and typed those messages.

Even if I had control of my hands, I'm not sure I could have held on emotionally. I'm not sure my parents could have either. My parents had already witnessed the horror of me getting hurt and lying motionless on the field, crying in terror through a muffled scream because I couldn't operate my diaphragm.

But my brother handled the overwhelming emotion as he dialed the phone, held it in front of my face, and then dialed again and again over a thirty-minute stretch. He held the phone through three calls. The first was to Tyler Douglas, who had our fellow friend Chase Bixby with him.

Tyler and I were best friends and college workout partners on the rugby team. We lifted and trained together. We knew each other's goals and aspirations. On a nearly daily basis, I could tell you almost down to the ounce what Tyler weighed because we were charting each other's dreams. It must have been so painful for him to see me utterly broken after all the time we spent building each other up.

Then there was Jack Iscaro, who was joined by Agustin Centurion, and finally, Nick Econome. Each call lasted roughly five minutes and followed a pattern. I explained that I was almost completely paralyzed from the neck down. As the doctor had told me, I told them I would probably never walk again, and if I was lucky, I might be able to feed myself. Eating a slice of pizza would be an accomplishment.

All of that was *if* I survived the surgery. I finished by telling each of them once more that I loved them, saying what could be my final goodbye. Next, my brother typed a message to a group I met through a high school Catholic retreat. I let them know what had happened and asked for their prayers.

Finally, there was a group message to all my teammates. Rugby is a game of collective struggle where teammates bond over the willingness to endure pain for each other. That willingness to sacrifice is unbreakable, and we were the best. I spoke while my brother typed:

> Hey guys. First off, congratulations on a hell of a win. I couldn't be more proud! Currently I'm paralyzed below the chest, unable to move at all and the possibility of me being able to play rugby or even walk is very low. I love you all and it's been a hell of

a ride and I'm proud to call you all my family. Any prayers would be much appreciated and I will truly miss playing with all of you.

Love, Robert Paylor

I noticed my brother wipe away a tear only occasionally. He never showed what was going through his mind or let the emotion of the moment get the best of him. I needed that so badly as I did my best to beat back the pain, anxiety, and terror of feeling almost completely disconnected from my body.

My brother was the champion of the moment as I opened my heart again and again to the people I could think of in this chaotic time. I was focused on what I needed to do next, which was to prepare for the possibility that these were my last moments on earth.

When you expose your emotions and experience such deep pain, the tears flow like water from a broken washing machine. After repeating that process four or five times, you're completely drained. While this may be an overused laundry analogy, I wasn't only put through the wringer emotionally, I felt like I had the washing machine dropped on me.

Even with painkillers, my neck throbbed with excruciating pain. The doctor returned to get my final decision. Again, this was a formality. The only thing I asked was that we wait for the priest to arrive and lead my family in prayer.

In the meantime, there was a little ceremony to conduct. My mom retrieved my championship medal after my teammates had finished off the victory. She brought it to me so I could wear it as a champion at least one time.

I had spent years dreaming of playing rugby for Cal. This day was supposed to be about triumph and legacy. When she laid it on my chest, I couldn't do anything but cry. I had envisioned wearing this medal earlier in the day. I never imagined I would wear it like this.

When the time came, Father Michael Tyrrell, a priest, entered the room and led my parents, my brother, and me in prayer. He gently anointed my forehead and hands with oil for the Sacrament of Anointing of the Sick. I prayed silently, desperate for God's healing and forgiveness. I loved my life and all the people around me. I couldn't bear the thought of this being my last day. We then prayed the Lord's Prayer together, and I recited Psalm 23, just as I had done hours earlier before my last rugby game.

> Even though I walk through the valley of the shadow of death, I will fear no evil, for you are with me; your rod and your staff comfort me. You set a table before me in front of my enemies; you anoint my head with oil; my cup overflows. Indeed, goodness and mercy will pursue me all the days of my life; I will dwell in the house of the Lord for endless days.

I said goodbye to my mom, dad, and brother. There were tears, but no hugs. As desperately as I wanted to be held or hold them, it wasn't happening. I had to remain as still as possible. Turning my neck could have meant extinguishing the remaining sliver of hope I had of ever moving again.

The tiny threads of nerves that made up my spinal cord had already been severed or frayed by the trauma of my neck snapping. Anything beyond a kiss on the forehead was too risky.

The nurses came to wheel me into the operating room.

I had to keep pushing forward. I had to drive out all fear. I had to control my mindset. While I obviously survived the surgery, I was a long way from being out from under the shadow of death. Over the next month, the real fight for my life would begin.

The juxtaposition of this day is not lost on me. When I woke up that morning, it was going to be the day I established my legacy at Cal as a champion. Throughout the years I played at Jesuit High School in Sacramento, home to the winningest high school rugby program in America, we were never able to win a national championship while I was on the varsity team. It slipped through my grasp like sand through my fingers.

I played other sports in high school, such as football. I could have played small-college football or at a lower-level NCAA Division I program, but that wasn't really what I wanted to chase. Education was my priority, and I loved rugby more than football.

Cal was the perfect combination of a top-tier education and elite athletics. UC Berkeley is the number one ranked public university in the world and one of the most competitive schools in the country. I planned to get into the Haas School of Business at Cal. The department looks favorably on athletes because of our competitive spirit and discipline. Rugby was going to help me succeed in practically every facet of life I could envision. I gave to the game, and it gave to me.

I became a starter on the varsity team as a sophomore, a rare accomplishment in itself. I had the size, and I loved the contact. I lived for it. My position was tighthead lock, which is similar to a tight end in football.

Guys like me are the workhorses. We put our bodies in places where others don't. We use our finesse in the lineouts and our strength to drive the other team backward. We live for what are called mauls, rucks, and scrums.

The maul can be a dark and treacherous place where people push themselves to physical extremes in what is one of the greatest collective feats of strength in sports. Sometimes it is a dirty place where the play of the game can cross the line if the officials are not careful.

That's what happened to me.

I woke up that morning thinking it would be the best day of my young life. It was a day that would define me in many ways. It did just that, but not in the way I had anticipated when I got out of bed. It was a beautiful, partly cloudy day in Santa Clara. We were an extraordinarily effective team. I was confident we were going to win. Once you become a national champion, you are a national champion forever.

I briefly thought about the final exams I had to take later in the month and the internship I had waiting for me at Intel. Just that week, I had talked to my internship manager. I told her I was raring to go and would be there shortly after winning this title.

I had slept reasonably well, aside from the usual pregame jitters. Every moment I wasn't warming up for the game, I was resting to make sure my body was in a maximum state of preparation. The butterflies in my stomach told me I was ready for a full eighty minutes of continuous, full-contact competition.

I vividly remember putting on my rugby socks, shorts, T-shirt, and Cal tracksuit. It would be the last time I got dressed so easily. I ate breakfast, silently focusing on the game. Then there was a team meeting. There wasn't any yelling or screaming to get ourselves jacked up. It was just a final session to talk through the game plan and review our preparation. There is a been-there, done-that approach for the Cal program because that's who we are. We were competing for what would become our thirty-first national title since the college championship game began in 1980.

We entered the game fully prepared. We knew Arkansas State's strengths and weaknesses. We knew what to watch out for and what to exploit. We had lost only one match to an American team that year and by a very thin margin. We were a machine, built on generations of men striving for excellence.

I always kept that perspective in mind. I was a small part of something much bigger than myself. I didn't play for my individual glory. I played for my teammates, my coaches, our university, and our supporters. Many people had worn the blue and gold of Cal before me, and I felt a responsibility to them.

Our coaches talked about upholding a standard that had been set for decades and would continue for years to come. That's an essential part of team building. You're not just doing it year to year. You're doing it generation to generation. For Cal Rugby, that standard has also played itself out away from the field.

Cal Rugby isn't just a sports team. It sets a standard of excellence and carries the responsibility to live up to it. As we walked from our hotel to our bus for the short trip to our match at Santa Clara University, we knew we were going there to uphold something we all felt a sacred bond to. I dreamed that one day in the future when I had a wife and kids, I would bring them back to show them I was a part of something unique and great.

As we got closer to game time, our focus grew more intense. Again, no one spoke much. My thoughts about final exams and the Intel internship vanished. None of that mattered. It was time to be in the moment. During our warmup, we were sharp. We were never overly strenuous in warmups, but you could tell we were ready to click.

After that, we all put on our jerseys. If you're a starter in rugby, your number corresponds to your position. I was number 5. Everyone who plays rugby and wears number 5 is a tighthead lock. It's like a fraternity within the sport itself.

Again, tighthead locks have a particularly strong appetite for contact. You don't just react to it, you seek it. As the game goes on, you wear people down. I loved not only the contact in rugby, I loved the endurance required to maintain that level of contact. You want to make your opponent quit.

Associate head coach Tom Billups helped me pull my jersey over my head and gave me a firm pat on the back as we got ready. We stood tall as the national anthem played over the loudspeakers. I enjoy the anthem and what it represents. I hoped I could muster an ounce of courage the soldiers who sacrificed for our country had shown in keeping our nation free.

I know people have an image of Cal as a center of liberalism and progressive ideology. It's a diverse place of free and open thought. I didn't necessarily fit the image of what outsiders think represents Cal, but I fit in at Cal and that's what I cared about. We huddled up for the last time after the anthem and then lined up for the kickoff.

As I always did, I recited Psalm 23 to myself. We waited for the referee to raise his arm and blow his whistle. As that high-pitched sound pierced the air, we kicked the ball to Arkansas State and sprinted downfield. For me, it was the last time I would ever run like that.

Within the first minute, Arkansas State committed a

penalty, and we gained possession within seven meters of the goal. This is where the game becomes a maul. The larger players bind together as a single unit to drive the ball for a score against the opponent. This was where I excelled. This was where we were lethal against our opponents.

This was where my life changed.

REFLECTION QUESTIONS

1. What emotion, mental block, or challenging circumstance is paralyzing you from achieving your goal?

2. How would you act differently if you weren't affected by fear, frustration, or fatigue?

3. What is one immediate, positive action you can take today to break free from what's paralyzing you and move closer to your goal?

Chapter 2

BUILD A FOUNDATION

Robert had every reason to not show up and work as hard as he did, and certainly not in front of fellow student-athletes who had seen him before. But that's not how he thinks and who he is. It's pretty much who he has always been. He was like that before he was injured, and the injury has made it more obvious and apparent for the world to see.

—TOM BILLUPS, ASSOCIATE HEAD COACH, CAL RUGBY

A T TWELVE YEARS old, I unknowingly began preparing for my battle with quadriplegia.

Whether we realize it or not, every decision we make contributes to building our foundation to stand against the trials of life. Consider it your mental toughness or ability to respond constructively to pain. Storms of adversity will strike. Our ability to respond depends on the strength of the foundation we've built.

When we persevere through adversity and seek out discomfort, we grow and build a foundation of rock, ready to withstand the strongest storms. When we shy away from challenges outside our comfort zone, we build a foundation of sand, which can be swept away by the lightest breeze.

I never anticipated my foundation would face the Category 5 hurricane of quadriplegia, but I distinctly remember the day when my understanding of preparation and effort changed.

Practicing with the Oak Ridge Junior Trojans football team is my proof.

It may sound silly to some that a moment practicing youth sports could be life-altering, but it's true for me. It's imprinted on my brain as the day the switch flipped for me. I had an overwhelming emotional response to how my life was going.

It triggered a physical reaction that evolved into a mental approach to life. I wasn't going to settle for the mediocre effort I had been putting in. I wasn't going to let my opportunities escape me. I decided to embrace discomfort and take on challenges with passion.

This moment became a touchstone for everything from playing rugby at the highest level to aspiring to attend the best college I could. When rugby ended in tragedy, this moment became the starting point to survive the greatest challenge of my life.

These days, I can only begin to explain how important it is to embrace difficult circumstances and pour full effort into every endeavor. This is not just about physical preparation, like doing push-ups or sit-ups to get in shape.

It's not just about learning a playbook as an athlete, studying a script as an actor, or conducting experiments as a scientist. Preparation is also about the mental willingness to undertake a difficult process.

Dozens of catchphrases emphasize this point. The classic is the "road less traveled." My Cal Rugby coaches would talk about going into that "dark closet" in your mind to overcome the exhaustion and pain of training and competing. Football coach Jim Harbaugh has used the phrase "make it suck" to encourage players to practice as hard as they can so that the game becomes easy.

Once I was injured and had to fight the tormenting thought that I might never walk again, I asked myself: How am I going to change the course of my life now that my physical abilities have changed? How am I going to find a way to succeed?

I thought back to that day at youth football practice. That's why I always tell people to prepare now. Face your challenges and build a strong foundation. Face the difficult mental task of preparing for hardship. Do it *now*. It doesn't matter what age you are, give it your all.

I was lucky that the moment happened early.

By age twelve, I was in my third year of trying to play football. I say "trying" because there hadn't been much success at that point, even though I was the biggest and strongest kid on the team. For whatever reason, I didn't have the aggression that the game requires. It was so obvious when I was ten that I got cut in the first week of tryouts. I didn't even make it to a practice.

I didn't hate football. I just didn't love it. But I knew how much my dad loved the game. He was a football fan and had played in high school. He thought the game would be useful for me, teaching me about toughness, discipline, and aggression. So, I spent the next year working on my conditioning and strength, determined to make the cut when I was eleven.

I got through tryouts this time, but I still had no passion. I was on the team, but not really playing. My dad tried to help me unleash my passion. He would give me pep talks as we drove to practice in his white Ford Taurus company car. He always encouraged me. Still, I could tell it was tinged with his belief that I wasn't getting enough out of myself.

My dad would talk about how much potential I had. He tried to rephrase the message as time went on. He talked about my "capabilities" or my "gifts." My dad tried every synonym imaginable for the word potential. I love him for that and I know how hard he was trying.

I also know plenty of other parents struggle with how to get through to their kids. I'm sure I'm going to be in the same position someday, trying to figure out how to motivate my child, wondering whether my message is getting through.

What got through to me was underneath what my dad was saying. I wasn't giving enough. I wasn't using my gifts. He tried to dress it up nicely, but it was the inescapable truth.

Then he tried other tactics. He'd slip in some heavy metal, power chord rock and roll hoping to get me in the right mindset to bang my body around in practice. There was some Metallica, AC/DC, and probably even a little Black Sabbath mixed in. I'm not sure the folks at our Catholic church would exactly relate to the musical choices, but my dad was trying anything he could.

All it really did was make me fall in love with the music. Then my dad tried to get me to use my imagination to conjure up some aggression for practice. He would turn to Luke in his effort to fire me up.

Not the Gospel of Luke, mind you. Rather, Luke the cat. Both of them were close to my heart, but Luke the cat certainly had a more personal connection.

Luke was our family cat. Luke was big and black. Not fat, just big. He had a tall, wide frame and a muscular stature. When people came to our house, they would say he looked like a miniature panther roaming the yard.

Luke also had the personality of a dog. He'd always come up to greet people. When we came home from being out, Luke ran to us, meowing loudly until we picked him up.

While he loved everyone, I was definitely his favorite. On the days when my brother wasn't around, Luke would walk around the property with me. He was one of the few cats I've known who would actually come whenever I called. We were inseparable.

To get me motivated, my dad would tell me to imagine that whoever I was playing against had stolen Luke. It's a common sports cliché. Plenty of athletes picture their opponents as villains to ignite their competitive fire. I get the idea. It just didn't work for me. Never did. Never has.

I think part of the problem was a funny contradiction in my dad's messages. Most of the time, he told me to be kind to everybody at school or whenever I met new people.

My parents have worked in sales for over twenty years. They are great with people and understand the power of personal relationships. They know how to treat others with courtesy. They understood that because of my stature and personality, I could impact a lot of people and do a lot of good. By the time I was in high school, I was the captain of the football team and the director of the band, two groups that don't always have a lot in common. I could bring people together.

At age eleven, I had a hard time differentiating aggression in competition from being kind to everyone in day-to-day life. I didn't know how to translate the difference. To this day, I've never hated an opponent. My passion and drive were always about loving the game and the competition.

Put it together and what you have is a young me who was just kind of going through the motions in youth football. The turning point came when I was twelve and another kid was playing ahead of me on the offensive line. He was my friend, but he wasn't as big or as athletic as me. Frankly, I knew he wasn't as good as me.

One day as we drove to practice, I remember feeling fed up. I was fed up with the whole situation. I was fed up with the coaches who thought the other kid was better than me. I was fed up with not understanding my dad's pep talks, blaring metalhead music, and imagery about somebody stealing Luke.

Most of all, I was fed up with myself.

Here I was, years into the process and countless practices later, and I knew I wasn't giving it my all. I was playing, but I wasn't playing with passion. That day, I decided it was time to live up to my potential. It was time I finally practiced and played with desire.

I told myself that I was going to do whatever it took to put my friend on his back all practice and show everyone I was better. Not just better than him. I was better than what I had been putting out. I was better than what my coaches had witnessed to this point.

I started yelling during practice and giving maximum effort. I was disrupting every play, tackling the running back behind the line of scrimmage and sacking the quarterback on pass plays. At one point, the coaches went up to my dad and asked if I was mentally OK and if everything was all right at home.

As practice went on and I kept dominating my friend who was starting in front of me, the coaches eventually threw in the towel on trying to stop me. They told the other kid to just dive at my legs when I lined up because there was no way he or anybody else was going to stop me. In just one practice, I became a starter.

That part of the equation was crucial. The payoff for my effort was immediate and that fueled me. I eventually became a standout player and a captain. In high school, I was first-team all-league and recruited to play at the collegiate level. I went from being cut at age ten to becoming the type of player everyone would remember. I saw that if I gave everything I had, I would get recognized and rewarded.

It was the same thing in class. If I put more effort into studying and working hard, I would earn better grades. I became competitive in school and started to realize that I could chase bigger dreams, such as going to a school like Cal. My effort that one day in practice opened up a world of possibilities.

After I was paralyzed, I understood the kind of effort I had to exert to survive both mentally and physically.

The concept of giving maximum effort evolves as challenges grow tougher over time. It's one thing to outplay your twelve-year-old buddy in youth football. It's another to compete for a starting spot for the best college rugby program in the United States.

It's even harder to survive the physical and mental trauma of being paralyzed. As you go through life and compete at a higher level with more talented people or with more on the line, the challenges amplify.

I was fortunate to live that out. When I got to high school, I played football and basketball as a freshman. At six foot five, it was evident I had a future in football. Basketball was another story. I developed my skills a lot as a freshman, but there was one guy who was six foot eight and another who was six foot ten playing center on the varsity team, each of them a year older than me. They were both standouts who went on to play college basketball.

It didn't take a visionary to see that my hoop dreams were going to be limited to backup status. Not that I'm a prima donna, but if I was playing a sport, I wanted to actually play. I looked around for other options. I had played baseball too, but I didn't see a future in that either.

In the middle of my sophomore year, I discovered the Jesuit High School rugby team.

Rugby was a spring sport, and Jesuit was a national powerhouse. At the time, the school had won six national titles and finished runner-up three times in the previous fifteen years. We won the national championship in my sophomore year and were runner-up in my junior and senior years when I was on the starting team. Since I graduated, they have won two more titles.

The other enticing aspect of Jesuit rugby was that it was a pipeline to playing for Cal. It seemed like every year two or three players were recruited from Jesuit to Cal. While Cal didn't provide financial scholarships for rugby, the edge Jesuit rugby gave me to get into a prestigious school like Cal was enticing.

I was a good student and finished high school with a 4.0 weighted grade-point average, but that doesn't cut it at Cal by itself. I needed the edge that rugby provided. More than anything, I wanted to be part of an organization that set a standard of excellence. When it comes to rugby, the Jesuit and Cal programs are unmatched.

There was just one big problem when I got started with rugby: I didn't understand how to play. In football, a typical play lasts five or six seconds, the whistle blows, you go back to the huddle, catch your breath, get the next call, and repeat. It's all these short bursts of extreme energy and contact, then recovery time.

While rugby shares football's physicality, its structure of play is entirely different. In rugby, you play continuously like in soccer. You have two forty-minute halves with a fifteen-minute halftime break. There are also no rolling substitutions like in hockey, basketball, or other popular American sports. Once you're substituted out, you can't go back in.

As a sophomore on the junior varsity team, I played in my first intrasquad scrimmage. I wanted to immediately prove myself as an athlete, so I operated in my all-out, twelve-year-old style. I sprinted all over the field. I launched my body into every tackle. I chased every ball carrier like an overexcited Labrador retriever.

After two minutes, I was exhausted, wheezing with my hands on my knees. I thought I was about to faint. I only had thirty-eight more minutes to go in the first half.

I quickly figured out that energy was a finite commodity that had to be used strategically in this game. This was a completely different sport in terms of conditioning, and I was going to have to change my training approach. My all-out strategy had to change.

This is what I mean about how the challenge changes. This wasn't youth football anymore, where I could rely on my size and effort to overpower opponents. I still had to give maximum effort, but I had to use my brain.

Then, of course, there was the physical aspect. Again, the collisions in rugby are similar to those in football, but the lack of padding changes technique and removes any sense of protection. There's no way to get around the fact that if an opponent outweighs you by fifty pounds and he's running full steam at you, it's going to hurt. You have to learn to embrace the discomfort and sacrifice.

That sacrifice was rewarded by the support I received from my high school coach. Coach John Shorey, who led Jesuit High School to ten national titles in his twenty-three years, fed my passion. Shorey is the kind of man who can be both a coach and a friend.

I would have run through walls for Shorey. He was that way for a lot of guys. The Jesuit program was a no-cut program because he wanted everybody to have the opportunity to develop and contribute.

He also created a vision for me. He would talk about how I would one day be an Eagle, which is the name for the USA Rugby Men's National Team. I ate it up. It made me want to practice harder and harder. If you want to look at it another way, making it suck in practice was easy for me because of the vision Shorey planted in my head.

That mental desire to put everything on the line continued to pay off early in my senior year at Jesuit. I got a call from Cal's rugby program, inviting me for a recruiting trip. Simply being considered for the Cal program was mentally intoxicating. I was also being recruited by some other schools for rugby and a couple of schools for football. But the dream was always about going to Cal and getting into the Haas School of Business. When my parents and I visited, I was immediately sold.

Standing at six foot five with a voice that projects with authority, Coach Clark commands a colossal presence. His reputation precedes him with twenty-nine national championships in his coaching career, and he also isn't a guy who minces words. He doesn't tell you what you want to hear. He tells you what you need to hear. He was straightforward as he talked about my potential and how going to Cal would give me the chance to fully access that potential—a concept that now registered with me after all those pep talks from my dad.

I'll get more into the story of Cal Rugby and what the program means later. Just understand that rugby is the first varsity sport at Cal and has won thirty-three national championships as I write this book. The rugby-dedicated field is pristine, tucked in the hills surrounding Strawberry Canyon and overlooking the San Francisco Bay. It's a bona fide Division I collegiate athletic experience.

This was what I wanted to be part of, and I can trace my ascension to being considered by Cal to that moment when I was twelve. Once I got into Cal, the challenge became even larger. My teammates weren't guys I could just overpower. These were some of the most talented and hardworking players in the country.

The concept of "giving it your all," "taking the road less traveled," "going into that dark closet," "making it suck," or whatever phrase rings true in your head takes on new meaning.

For me, that was about training. I was never the most skilled player in terms of ball-carrying or passing. I was a workhorse who was expected to win at the point of contact and secure the ball for the players who scored. This demanded exceptional strength, endurance, and mental toughness. If I was going to make it, I had to maximize those abilities. I had to develop my endurance to withstand the roughest situations.

At Cal, I became best friends with Tyler Douglas, who I played against in high school. Tyler doesn't let me forget that his team beat us our senior year. Whatever. We overcame that and became workout partners. We drove each other. Tyler pushed me to put in extra work because I knew he was counting on me to be at the gym. It was like having an accountability partner.

We would work out for an additional hour and a half on top of the training we did with the team. In the summers, our goal was to reach a level of extreme discomfort as the lactic acid built and burned in our muscles. If either of us woke up the next day and didn't feel sore, we were disappointed. That meant we hadn't worked hard enough. That was unacceptable.

We sometimes pushed ourselves to the point of vomiting. There were many times we'd be doing an exercise, one of us would run to the bathroom to puke and then come back to finish the set. That level of exertion might sound crazy, but it was about the payoff. I wasn't the fastest guy on the team, but there were plenty of times that you'd see me running downfield late in games, able to keep pushing when others tired out.

Another payoff came during practices. I'd make a good play in practice, and Coach Clark would shout, "It looks like someone wants to be a starter this year!" Receiving a compliment of that degree from him wasn't an everyday occurrence. That's a feeling I got addicted to.

But the biggest payoff came when I faced the fight for survival. Whether it was the level of pain I experienced from the injury, the fear of whether I would survive, or the exhaustion of the treatments that lay ahead, I was prepared. I was prepared for the dark places I went to in my mind.

I was prepared for a road I hope no one else has to travel.

Reflection Questions

1. When have you overcome adversity before, and what tools did you use that could help you now?

2. What aspects of your life reflect a foundation built on sand, and how can you start rebuilding with rock?

3. What decision can you make today that your future self will thank you for?

Chapter 3

CREATE A VISION

The only thing worse than being blind is having sight but no vision.

—HELEN KELLER

A S MY MIND and body were stretched to their limits by injury, I got my first lesson in figuratively stretching a rubber band.

I've been stretching that rubber band as far as it can go ever since.

There's a simple exercise that illustrates the concept of vision. In particular, a grand vision. A vision that's so ambitious most people can't comprehend the process of turning it into reality.

I learned this exercise in a class at Cal taught by Professor Dan Mulhern, a great public speaker and leadership advisor. But I lived the exercise before I learned it, as Mulhern pointed out one day in class.

Let's start with the exercise. Take a rubber band, loop it around your thumbs, then hold your left thumb steady while stretching your right thumb to the right as far as it will go. As the tension builds, the right thumb is trying to pull the left thumb along. Hold that left hand steady.

Then take a good look and understand that your right hand represents your vision, the place where you want to be. The left hand represents where you are today. The tension represents the steps and difficulty of getting there.

The farther your right hand is stretched, the bigger the vision and the larger the tension. Our ability to hold that tension determines our success. We often resist big ideas because they seem too daunting. We hear people talk about the pitfalls of trying to build a business or climb a mountain and we get scared.

Then there are the people who think big. They see the world differently. They take that rubber band and stretch it until the middle of the band starts to fray. They have no fear that the band will snap. They're able to hold that tension, no matter how strong it is.

That's like John F. Kennedy proposing that the United States race the Soviet Union to put a man on the moon. It's Henry Ford in the auto industry, Dr. Dre in music, or any one of Steve Jobs, Bill Gates, or the founders of Google in the technology field.

Or, in my case, the notion that I will one day walk again. I believe I will walk again, and I saw it in a lucid dream I had the day after my emergency surgery. I believe I will walk again because I relentlessly work every day in pursuit of my vision.

I believe in it because I have learned to stretch that rubber band. I know the steps. I see the process. I understand the importance of what I'm doing, especially how important it is to others.

And yes, I'm realistic. I knew that my chances of ever moving again were about 3 percent or less based on the initial estimate the doctors gave me. Again, that was just to be able to move something, not get up and walk. The odds of walking were probably 1 percent, if that.

I also understand that even if I never fully walk, success

lies as much in the journey as in the destination. I know that, if nothing else, the pursuit of my ultimate goal will motivate me to make the most of my life. As author and management consultant Robert Fritz said, "It's not what the vision is, it's what the vision does."

This is the power of vision and purpose.

I intuitively understood that the day I got hurt. As my doctor described the physical limitations that would define my life, I kept thinking, "That's not enough." I wasn't going to be satisfied simply lifting a piece of pizza to my mouth.

Eating pizza is not a life goal. That's not *doing* something with my life in a way that makes a difference in the world. It's not an accomplishment grounded in a sense of purpose the way I had been raised to believe.

I wasn't put on earth to eat a slice of pizza. I was put on earth to impact lives. I was put here to move people. I needed something to fight for, and that wasn't going to be easy.

After I woke up from surgery, I lay there groggy, squinting as the yellow artificial light beamed toward my eyes. My ears were bombarded by the constant beeping of medical equipment tracking my vitals. My body was numb and limp. Yesterday wasn't a bad dream that I would simply wake up from. This was real.

A new doctor visited me. He was much more optimistic, which I needed.

First, he gave me a rundown of the surgery. He explained that they removed my ruptured disc and replaced it with an artificial one. They also fused my two broken vertebrae, which left lots of space for regeneration of my spinal cord and relieved pressure from the area.

I immediately asked if I was going to be able to walk

35

and move my hands again. He said probably not, but left a sliver of hope. He said these injuries were catastrophic and chronic, so the odds were not in my favor. At the same time, he said I had a couple of positives going for me. The first was that I was young and my nervous system was still developing. There were many studies showing that being younger increases the odds of having a higher degree of neurological recovery.

The second was that I was an athlete. My body was already in shape. My blood circulation was good. My heart was strong. I was in better shape to take on the medical challenges that would come my way (not knowing the first challenge was only hours away).

Finally, being an athlete gave me a mindset that would help in those challenging moments. In short, he gave me the opportunity to ask the classic *Dumb and Dumber* rhetorical question: "So, you're telling me there's a chance?"

I wasn't throwing a celebration, but considering the circumstances, I felt better. At this point, I was utterly exhausted, and I was on a lot of medication because I was still in excruciating pain. I'm pretty sure it was the middle of the night or really early in the morning because my family and friends weren't there to visit yet. They weren't allowed in my room at night because of ICU regulations.

That's when I dozed off and had this incredibly lucid dream that has helped carry me to this day. I had experienced lucid dreams before, where I realized I was dreaming and could do anything I imagined. There were dreams when I believed I was flying, and I actually felt the air rushing by me.

In this dream, all I wanted was to sprint. I could feel my muscles contract as I ran. I cherished the sensation of my legs blasting my body forward with every stride, my arms ripping back and forth, and the wind streaming by my face.

Then I started to do footwork drills like the ones I had done in rugby and football. I spent the whole dream running, standing up, and loving the ability to move my body and feel the sensation. It was euphoric and inspiring. It was counter to everything that my doctors were telling me about my future. It was everything I needed to fight for.

More than two years later, after I spent that time healing and rehabilitating my body, I sat in Mulhern's class one day and was asked to explain my vision. It was, as Mulhern put it, one of those drop-the-mic moments.

"It's so funny how reciprocal that moment was," Mulhern says. "The day that Rob delivered his story, that drop-the-mic meme was at the top of its glory. I think it was maybe the third class of the semester because I remember literally saying to the class, 'If you got that, nothing else I say the rest of this semester will really matter or be substantive.' What Rob was talking about was the whole point of what I was trying to teach."

When I first created my vision, I had no idea how to make it a reality, and I had doctors tell me that it likely would never happen. If you want to talk about the tension of a stretched rubber band, it doesn't get much stronger than that. But under that tension, it's also important to stay realistic about your starting point.

I was always very in tune with the severity of my injury. I knew how high the odds were stacked against me and how much time and effort it was going to take to beat those odds. That expectation only motivated me to work harder. I met others who weren't as grounded.

Many patients I met with injuries like mine would say, "I'm not a quadriplegic, and I won't spend the rest of my life in a wheelchair. That just isn't me. I'll be walking out of this hospital in a month." Since these patients weren't honest about their current reality, they didn't take their rehab as seriously, and as a result, they didn't see any improvement. That's why having a solid understanding of your starting point and a well-developed plan are integral parts of your vision.

Eventually, you'll reach the point when you've stretched the rubber band and have your ambitious vision. You're looking at your left hand and know where you're starting. You pan over to your right hand and can see your vision clearly and distinctly. You'll do whatever it takes to turn it into reality.

Now what?

This is where you have to think from right to left. Mulhern calls that "TRTL," pronouncing it "turtle" to make it easier to remember.

This is a process that goes against the traditional way many of us in Western culture think. We see the world the way we read and write, from left to right, and in the sense of a timeline, from present to future. We think in terms of making incremental, step-by-step improvements from where we are now, such as losing five or ten pounds on a diet or getting a 3 or 5 percent raise at our job.

That's not to say the left-to-right incremental approach is ineffective. As the saying goes, a journey of a thousand miles begins with one step. At the same time, we often get caught up in the idea of only making our present-day steps and lose sight of the end goal of our vision.

When Professor Mulhern describes the process of thinking right to left, it's about understanding the tension in the rubber band. Again, that tension represents all the steps and maneuvers required to accomplish the vision.

As you stretch that rubber band and establish your vision, you likely won't foresee every step or obstacle ahead. You probably don't know the pitfalls or investments you're going to have to make. But it's important you don't embark on your vision blindly. Use the system of thinking from right to left to plan out the steps required to achieve your desired outcome.

Begin with your vision on the far right. Then, work backward one step from right to left to visualize the milestone that needs to be accomplished right before you achieve your end goal. Make a note of it, and then take another step to the left, note the milestone, and then repeat the process until you have mapped out each of the steps required to turn your vision into reality, in sequence from right to left, ending at the current moment. It's quite a process, but this approach orients our steps around the end goal, always keeping us focused on that ultimate vision, not lost in near-term challenges.

My end goal since day one has been to not need my wheelchair again. Thinking from right to left, I'll need to be able to walk at least a mile before my vision is accomplished. Before that, I'll need to be able to stand up from the ground. Before that, I'll need to be able to open doors for myself. The cycle continued on and on until I reached my current reality—lying in a hospital bed, recovering from surgery.

As visiting hours began on Sunday, May 7, 2017, my extended family, teammates, and friends came to Santa Clara. I probably had a dozen family members drive in from Sacramento and Reno and maybe thirty friends make the hour drive from Berkeley to check on me. I needed every bit of their support.

When they came into the room, they expected to see

a broken version of me. Paralyzed, depressed, and barely holding on. What they saw was the same person I always was. Upbeat, joking around, and driven to accomplish my goals. The only difference was I couldn't move.

For me, it was an escape from it all. I was stretched thin between constant visits from hospital staff and the anxiety of how much my life had just changed, but when I could see my friends, all of that vanished for a little while. It felt like I was back in my college room, cracking jokes and talking about rugby practice. In those moments, I could be a normal twenty-year-old again. It was exactly what I needed to recharge and realize that there was so much in my life that I still retained.

When they asked about my injury, I told them what the second doctor had said. I told them I understood the statistics weren't on my side, but there was a chance. So, I was going to continue to build on this vision. I wasn't just going to envision standing up and walking again; I was going through the whole process of rebuilding my body. I had an insatiable appetite to regain what I had lost.

My larger goal of walking was broken into smaller parts. I had to envision myself working on my mobility and improving my strength in different areas. Even if I couldn't move certain parts of my body, I had a mental image of contracting those muscles. I would start at the top of my nervous system and work my way down. I started with my shoulders. I still had a strong connection there, so I would do twenty reps of shrugging my shoulders.

I could lift my arms just slightly, so I would close my eyes, raise my arms a few inches, and curl my biceps. I then worked my mental imagery down to the muscles I couldn't move, like in my hands. I poured all my effort into trying to close my fingers into a fist. Then I would imagine doing sit-ups and crunching my abdominal muscles. I had a good sense of what all the muscles in my body were supposed to do, so I focused on each isolated muscle.

I visualized completing twenty reps for each part of my body. I imagined using my hamstrings to bend my legs at the knee. I imagined tightening my calves and pointing my feet down, eventually working my way down to my toes. I went to exhaustion. I would ask my nurses to bring my legs up to help me get the feeling of moving...anything to help advance my self-prescribed rehab. I was willing my nervous system to reconnect.

Even though I didn't see immediate progress, I had to keep my vision and hold the tension of the rubber band. Doing these exercises wouldn't guarantee any progress, but I knew that doing nothing guaranteed defeat.

As I was trying to do that, a huge complication hit me and caused my first month to be my greatest test of survival and endurance. On that first day, as my family and friends were there, I noticed phlegm building in my throat. I tried to cough it up. No matter how hard I tried, I couldn't generate enough force to clear my throat. I didn't have the strength in my diaphragm to take a deep breath and push out a forceful cough. I could see the look of concern on my teammates' faces as I lay there choking.

A nurse rushed in to clear my windpipe, pushing forcefully against my diaphragm with both hands, almost like performing CPR. But the issue kept cropping up. It became so constant that I couldn't accept any more visitors that day. This devastated me since there were so many people I didn't get to see. But I could sense the phlegm building quickly. After some testing and a couple of days, my doctors told me I had contracted pneumonia.

They said that it was aspiration pneumonia, which

means it was from some type of tiny object I breathed in. It could have been while I was lying on the field for so long struggling to breathe. Or there could have been some type of germ on the ventilator that went down my throat during surgery. It might have happened sometime between being taken from the field and then to surgery.

Nobody knows, and it didn't matter. I had pneumonia; therefore, I had a potentially deadly problem made worse by my physical condition. I couldn't get the phlegm out of my body. I was at serious risk of my lungs eventually collapsing and dying unless I could beat this illness.

I had to undergo breathing treatments every three hours. This was on top of the nurses who came in every two hours to rotate my body and make sure I didn't get bedsores. One of the top causes of death for people who become paralyzed is the infections they can develop from skin sores. That happens when blood circulation is cut off from the skin as someone lies or sits in the same position for too long.

Finally, the nurses also had to come in and check my vital signs every hour. My hospital room was like a revolving door as staff members rotated in and out to work on my body.

Between the constant breathing treatments, checks on my vital signs, and rolling my body to prevent skin sores, sleep was a luxury I couldn't afford. I barely managed to get two to four hours of sleep a day during the first two weeks after my injury.

It quickly got to the point where I craved getting just ten or fifteen minutes to doze.

Of all the challenges I've faced, none compared to the intensity of fighting pneumonia and enduring the grueling breathing treatments to clear my lungs. The treatments would last anywhere from twenty minutes to an occasional and brutal three-hour session. The nurses pushed on my diaphragm to help me cough up the constant buildup.

Even my entire nursing staff wasn't enough to keep me safe at all times. I wasn't their only patient, so they weren't always able to immediately clear my lungs. Mucus would clog my windpipe in an instant. I would lie there gasping for air, scared and desperate. Panic swept over me as I watched my oxygen levels plummet and my vision fade. I had never felt so helpless.

As the disease spread and covered the walls of my lungs, I wasn't getting enough air, so I needed a ventilator mask to help me breathe. Even with oxygen assistance, my body didn't have enough energy to sit upright, so I would pass out. I was forced to lie on my back. Even ten minutes of sitting in a chair was a feat.

My mom was by my side every hour the hospital staff would let her. She didn't just sit back and cry for help as I choked. She learned how to operate the machines and the technique for pushing on my diaphragm to keep me breathing. I can't imagine the emotions she felt as she pushed down with all her strength to keep me alive.

Every parent's worst nightmare is the thought of losing their child. My mom was living that nightmare, doing everything in her power to prevent it from becoming a reality.

Sometimes I might only cough up a quarter cup of phlegm. Sometimes it was a full cup. It was both disgusting and ominous to know how sick your body can become so quickly. I had probably four or five respiratory therapists on a quasi-rotation to perform the breathing treatments. I remember after one of them finished a particularly difficult treatment, he looked discouraged and worried.

As he left the room, he turned to me and said, "You're in trouble, Robert."

Was it the best thing to say? No. Was it a moment of human frailty for him? Yes. We all get there, and this therapist let it slip out. But it also was a reminder to me of what I was facing.

Death.

Death was sitting in that room, at my bedside, just waiting for me to surrender in the face of pain and fatigue.

That fatigue was worsened by the fact that I couldn't eat normally. At one point, I tried to just chew on some ice chips. As I swallowed, some of the ice and water went down my windpipe and caused me to choke. We discovered my neck and throat were so swollen from the injury and surgery that the flap that normally covers the windpipe when we swallow was unable to close. Normal eating was now impossible.

I entered the hospital as a six-foot-five, 240-pound young man. I took great pride in my stature and the presence it gave me. I remember the looks I would get when I walked into a room and people noticed my size. I had big, strong legs from working out for rugby. I loved building my body.

Now, I was watching my body quickly deteriorate because I could neither work out nor get enough nourishment. I lost sixty pounds that first month in the hospital. I was losing two pounds a day, and I could see it withering in front of my eyes. My once-toned legs were melting away like ice on a warm day. There was nothing I could do to stop it. All I could do was lie back helplessly and watch.

Still, I had to get some nourishment as I battled pneumonia. That required a feeding tube. Surgically inserting a tube directly into my stomach wasn't a great idea because of the increased chance of infection and the stress another procedure would have on my body. We had to go through my nose, back down my throat, and into my stomach to feed me a liquid diet of maybe 1,700 calories a day, if I could handle that.

The medical technician started by going through my nose. Sounds relatively simple, except I had broken my nose multiple times playing rugby. I had scar tissue and a deviated septum, which narrowed the nasal passage.

That made inserting the tube a bloody and painful process. The technician lubricated the narrow tube, put it in my nose a few inches, and then hit a blockage. The technician pushed harder and harder, jamming the side of my nasal passage and getting nowhere as I winced.

This wasn't just excruciating, it was bloody. Blood dripped down the back of my nose into my mouth. I could taste the warm, metallic flavor of my blood. As the technician pushed, the tissue in my nose became inflamed, making the process even harder. The technician spent twenty or thirty minutes just shoving and shoving this tube.

The process was repeated several times with the same results. The tube would go in a little farther, get stuck again, and then the pushing started. The pain was excruciating, but I stayed focused on how this had to get done. If I didn't eat, I would die.

This was all part of my vision for recovery and part of the extreme training I had gone through. This was the next most important thing I was facing. Whatever the pain was, it didn't matter. I had to control my mindset and get this done.

After two days of failed attempts, my nurses decided to have the procedure done under live X-ray. They assured me I would be under anesthesia, which was a huge relief after two grueling days of torture.

They were mistaken. There was no anesthesia, and it was one and a half hours of the most painful thing I've ever endured. After what felt like an eternity, they finally got the tube down my throat.

During the first week, my mom sat with me one evening, talking before she had to leave for the night. She told me she would do anything to take away my pain and had even prayed to God, begging Him to let her be the one paralyzed instead of me.

I told her that I could never wish for that to happen. I wouldn't allow this to be wished on anybody. You could name the worst person who's ever existed on this earth, and I wouldn't wish this on them. You can think of killers like Hitler or Genghis Khan, horrible souls who tormented people. I would not wish this experience on even them. I couldn't wish this suffering on any other human being.

It would be too cruel. Nothing I have ever done has compared to the complete pain and exhaustion I felt as I fought to keep death at bay. I fought for a simple future. I fought for the chance to get up on my feet again and just walk.

Amid all that darkness and suffering, the North Star that kept me moving in the right direction was my vision. I thought about it constantly. I was obsessed with being able to walk, breathe, and live independently again. I had an insatiable appetite to turn my vision into reality. No matter how much tension there was between my vision and current reality, I refused to waver.

I can't let go of the rubber band. I encourage you to hold on as well.

REFLECTION QUESTIONS

1. What is the ultimate vision for your life? Describe it vividly, reflecting on your passions, the legacy you want to leave, and the feelings you want to experience when your vision is achieved.

2. Being completely honest with yourself, what is your current starting point? What skills, knowledge, and resources do you lack to begin moving toward your vision?

3. Using the right-to-left approach, start with your vision as the destination. Working backward to your current reality, what milestones mark the path to turning your vision into reality? What specific actions or resources will you need at each milestone to move forward?

4. What is a daily action you can start working into your routine that will help you build momentum toward your vision?

Chapter 4
HAVE A MENTAL DIET

Rob, you have truly inspired me. I can't fathom what you have been through. I had a stroke in February [2021]. I have since altered my lifestyle. I walk every day. Every step I take, I don't think I can take another. Then I think of you...You are truly an inspiration to me.

—JOHN POTHIER, SURREY, BRITISH COLUMBIA

I EAT THIS KIND of message for breakfast.

When I talk about the "mental diet" and feeding yourself the positive messages that drive you to achieve your dreams or overcome hardships, the message from Pothier is a perfect example of what I mean.

It was the type of message I quickly learned to crave.

On top of the physical hell I endured after my surgery, I also feared what this would cost. Jennifer Douglas, the mother of my friend Tyler, was an angel and started a GoFundMe page to help raise money for my rehabilitation expenses.

While I was extremely grateful for the financial support, another vital element of the GoFundMe page was the donors' messages. Just three days after my injury, their words of encouragement began pouring in.

My brother, as he had done in the moments before my surgery, held my phone as I read the messages. I was exhausted from the pneumonia, the treatments, and the lack of sleep. Among the few things I had to look forward to was seeing my family and then reading these messages from friends, acquaintances, and, oftentimes, complete strangers. Some were simple messages of love and support. Some were deeper.

"Stay strong, Robert. Your challenge is greater than what most of us have to face in life, but so is the opportunity to show your character."

"Your experience has had a huge impact on our entire family. It reminds us that the everyday problems we complain about in life are really nothing at all. You are our inspiration to thank God for what we have, not what we don't have. You have determination and grit, and above all, a magnificent attitude. Attitude is everything. Along with devoted parents, friends, and unending prayers from all, you have many people in your corner. We're rooting for you and know that although you have a long road ahead, you will succeed. There is no doubt. We will not forget."

"Robert, we send you best wishes from New Zealand. You clearly have strong mana from what I've heard about you from coach Tom Billups. This is a hell of a challenge for you but a strong, resilient, good man like you will see it through. All the best."

"I played Cal Rugby 1984, 1985, third and then second string. I was never the athlete you are. Stay strong my friend. They say we are never given challenges we can't handle. When I see your superhuman abilities athletically, intellectually, socially, spiritually, I believe this to be true. Take care, please contact me if I can help you in any way. Cal Rugby is a team for life."

As I read those messages, I felt my soul being enriched, fueled by the love and concern of others. These people gave not only their money, which I desperately needed for short- and long-term medical expenses, but also their compassion.

I know some people may dismiss what I received as a result of my status. I was a college athlete competing in a high-profile game on a prominent team. My injury unfolded on national television. I benefited from a level of visibility not everyone gets. I understand that and I'm very grateful for it. But there is love and support out there no matter who you are, and you have to pursue it. You have to seek it out.

As I've learned from my own experience, you must continue seeking it out.

Those messages fueled me every day. I read them as soon as I could, and they made me realize I'm not just fighting for myself. I'm working on my recovery for those who need inspiration I can provide.

This has become a symbiotic relationship. People such as Pothier watch my daily workout videos and feel inspired. He talks about losing weight and getting in shape. It's incredibly touching:

> I never played rugby, but I'm a huge fan. I fell in love with the sport whilst channel surfing in the wee hours of Nov. 23, 2003, when I came across the World Cup final between England and Australia. An epic match it was. I'm always looking for rugby

to watch on TV. Pretty much anything, including US collegiate rugby.

I became aware of Robert's injury shortly after it happened in May 2017. I have followed Robert on Twitter for a few years and now started following him on Instagram. It's amazing to watch his progress.

I have a few health issues and mostly ignored doctors' warnings. I tipped the scales at 320 pounds on February 19, 2021. That was the day I had my stroke. It was a mini-stroke, but needless to say, it forced me to take a serious look in the mirror. I've had several MRIs, CT scans, and various tests to reveal a myriad of other health problems.

The first week after my stroke was brutal. I pretty much laid in bed for a week with a pounding headache. I had plenty of time on my hands. It was then I realized that if someone in Robert's condition could actually get out of bed again and walk, there shouldn't be any reason why I couldn't change my life.

I quit alcohol on April 8, 2021. That was when I turned 62. I changed my diet and took up walking. I post monthly on my progress on Instagram. I am currently walking more than 10 kilometers a day. My weight is down 110 pounds. I am feeling much better, but believe me, it is difficult to push myself every day to walk. I have arthritis in both knees. Every step is painful, but I stop and think about Robert, and my thought changes.

I can't begin to tell you what that means to me. It's the essence of my life. There's a certain selfishness to the whole operation now. I work out nearly every day and post my videos because I know the positive reaction they're going to get. Those reactions become breakfast for my mental diet.

I usually wake up at seven o'clock. The first thing I do is check my email to see what I have to do for work and clean up my inbox. Then I go straight to Instagram to check my messages. I either like or respond to everything on Instagram. I don't respond to everything on Twitter, but I respond to a lot. The positivity I get there feeds my mindset.

The other thing I did, especially early in my recovery, and still do quite a bit, was spend hours on YouTube watching videos of people overcoming paralysis or other disabilities. When I couldn't sleep or felt discouraged, I was very intentional about seeking stories that would fuel me.

I searched for "quadriplegic walks again" and scrolled through page after page, looking for stories like mine. These were people who suffered injuries and were told by doctors they'd never walk again, yet they fought anyway. They went through a journey, gave it everything they had, and then months or sometimes years later these people ended up on their feet. They encouraged me to believe it was possible and that I still had a chance.

I followed these people and their journeys. One was Chris Norton, who is another motivational speaker and has gone on to get married and have a family. I followed the journey of Rutgers football player Eric LeGrand, who was paralyzed in 2010 during a game. I love his mindset and positivity even though he hasn't seen the same degree of physical recovery due to the severity of his injury.

As I kept searching, I realized how essential it was to feed my mind with stories of others overcoming hardships. These days, my actions are a little more spontaneous in searching for stories like this on YouTube or Netflix, but it's still part of the intentional process of feeding my mental diet. Much of my time is spent sharing my own journey, so I can give that same boost to others.

It's important to feed that mental diet because there is so much that can get you down. I felt it when the first doctor told me I'd never walk again and would be lucky to feed myself. I understand that it was likely his way of being straight with me, but it was almost utterly without hope at a time when I was desperate for even the smallest sliver of promise.

I had to find a way to get out of that negativity. It was just like when my spiritual director reminded me that I had control over my mindset, and I had to shift my focus from mere survival to thriving again. This is what I mean by the mental diet. In many ways, it's not so different from a physical diet.

We all inherently know what's good for our bodies. We all know we shouldn't grab that bag of chips. We know we should put down that doughnut. We all know what's best for us, but we don't always do it. The same goes for our minds. We can recognize what's best for us if we have a constant audit of what's going on in our heads.

We have to ask ourselves, "Is this making me feel better or worse?" It's like people who meal prep. They are very intentional and habitual about what they put into their bodies.

It's the same with what we put into our minds. I know one person who said he was overwhelmed by the negative media of the 2020 US presidential election. It made him focus on the wrong things. It became a brain drain for him and made his attitude incredibly negative.

That is the kind of poison we allow into our minds

that takes us away from the task at hand and viewing the world in a more positive light. If you can't control a situation, don't let it control you. We have to let go of the things we can't change. Be aware of what you allow into your mind, and identify ways to remove anything toxic from your mental diet.

I know because the negativity gets to me. Each year on May 6, the anniversary of my injury, I have a hard time dealing with the day. I start to look at the clock and remember events. Reliving those moments is extremely difficult. Sometimes the only way I have been able to deal with it is to bury it in my mind. It feels like post-traumatic stress disorder for veterans who have witnessed the terrors of human behavior. They can't shake those memories or turn them into something positive, so they do what they can to repress them.

Reliving those moments can feel horrible. For the first fifteen months after my injury, I was so overwhelmed by trying to recover that I had to avoid reliving those moments no matter what. I had too much to focus on in terms of progressing or dealing with the immediacy of pneumonia, the injury, and my rehabilitation. I couldn't put myself in those memories of what happened because they would have broken me.

But as time has helped me recover, it has also brought those memories back to the surface. When May 6 arrives, I can't help but relive them. The memories are vivid, whether I want them to be or not. I remember waking up around eight o'clock, putting on my clothes with ease for the last time.

I hopped on a bus—the last time I walked onto a vehicle. I sat down and ate breakfast—the last time I sat in a normal chair for a meal. It all reminds me of every way that my life has changed, big and small.

I think about the moment when I was lying on the turf as the clock hit 1:00 p.m. In my mind, I can see the faces of the people who were looking at me. I can see the trainers running over. I can remember the sounds of the game going on around me and the terror within me. I remember sitting in that hospital bed, not knowing what was going to happen with my life. Lying in that MRI tube horrified, and then hearing the doctor tell me I would never walk or move my hands again.

I remember Father Tyrrell anointing my forehead and hands with oil during the Sacrament of Anointing of the Sick. I remember the phone call with my spiritual director about controlling my mindset and my brother holding up my phone so I could tell my friends I love them.

The memory that haunts me most is immediately after my injury when my parents came to see me on the field. I remember my dad grabbing my hand, and I could not feel it. My mom knelt right behind me and said, "We are right here. We will never leave you."

The only words I could get out with my choked-up voice were, "I love you more than anything in the world."

Reliving those moments engulfs my mind in negativity. I talk to my parents and my brother about it, and it brings back strong memories for all of us. But in that moment and in the process of getting past those memories, I am able to see what has happened these past eight years. Everything since that day has contributed to the personal pride I have from climbing out of that fateful juncture in my life.

I talk with my family and friends about being able to go back to Cal to graduate. We talk about the millions of people who have seen this journey and been inspired. We talk about individual stories of the people who have been impacted by my story.

As we talk about these positive moments, I get to choose what to focus on and carry forward from that day. I can allow my mind to keep swimming through these moments of tragedy, or I can focus on the positives and the sources of pride that greatly outnumber the negatives. It's not always easy, and I don't feel an immediate change in my mood, but as I focus on what I've retained and gained, my perspective gradually shifts.

As I have conversations with my family or other people close to me and they say, "Gosh, it's amazing how far you've come and all the incredible things that are ahead for you," it helps me refocus my mindset.

And understand this: I'm not searching for fleeting boosts to my mood. You hear the constant refrain from people, "How about hearing some good news?" They are looking for the happy little stories that you typically see on a morning news show, like a local cat being rescued from a tree or grandparents learning to TikTok.

That's fine, but I'm not looking for something sugary in my diet. Once in a while, sure. But that's not what builds a strong long-term mindset. That's not the kind of mental diet I want to create.

I want stories that uplift, but they have to begin with struggle before reaching the uplifting part. There's no way around that, and it's part of the conflict that goes with this mental diet. I hate how people have to endure pain and adversity. At the same time, I love to see them fight out of it.

It's so inspiring to me. It fuels my journey, reminding me that my situation could be so much worse and that my recovery is something so many other people have endured successfully.

Some of these stories are easier to handle than others. The movie *Bleed for This* is about boxer Vinny Pazienza coming back from a car crash that nearly killed him and almost left him paralyzed. Like me, Pazienza broke his neck, but he fortunately didn't have a spinal cord injury. He was advised to undergo surgery that would have ended his boxing career and forced him to give up his world title. Instead, in Rocky-esque style, Pazienza took a big risk to come back and defend his title.

I love that story, and Pazienza has reached out to me in the years since my injury, which was incredibly inspiring. At the same time, not all stories are quite that easy to digest.

One story in particular has stuck with me. It was a nine-minute video made in 2017 about John Hudson Dilgen. He was fifteen, suffering from epidermolysis bullosa (EB). It's awful, and to be frank, watching the video is very difficult. EB is a rare disorder where people lack type VII collagen in their bodies. This collagen is what makes your skin stick to your flesh.

Without type VII collagen, any force or friction makes the skin shear off. Simply rubbing against a wall or another person will cause skin to peel away. What it means is that Dilgen's body is essentially a giant open wound.

I remember when I used to get turf burns from playing rugby and complained about the stinging feeling of washing it. Dilgen lives with this feeling all the time over his entire body. He needs to be bandaged from his feet to his neck every day.

When he takes a bath, his entire body feels the sting of raw flesh against soap and water. He is reduced to tears and trembles in pain. He also can't eat solid food, as it would tear the skin in his esophagus. He can only have a liquid diet and depends on a series of medications to help him stay healthy.

Most newborns with EB don't survive. For those who do survive, they are usually exposed to terrible infections or, eventually, skin cancer. Their hands and feet also become disfigured over time. As I watched that video of Dilgen, it was incredibly hard to take in. But what I saw was this young man persevering. He maintains positivity and keeps fighting because he knows how much his life can inspire others. If he's capable of that despite the awful challenge he faces, I can fight to help others too.

Understanding this is essential for learning how to feed your mindset and keep yourself from wallowing in crippling mental pain.

Over the years, I've come across many books and programs that have helped shape my mindset. One of the most profound quotes I have incorporated into my public speaking is the one at the opening of this book from Viktor Frankl, the author of *Man's Search for Meaning*.

Frankl was an Austrian Jewish neurologist, psychiatrist, and philosopher, best known for his work on finding meaning through a purposeful mental attitude, particularly after he survived the Holocaust. I can't fathom the horrors Frankl survived, and I deeply admire the courage he had to remain in control of his mindset. It shows the power of the human spirit in the most extreme of circumstances.

Maintaining a positive mental diet is part of how I end my day, as well. This exercise started before my injury. When I attended Jesuit High School in Sacramento, we prayed the Prayer of Examen (also known as the Ignatian

Examen). Saint Ignatius of Loyola encouraged this practice as a way to develop a stronger connection with God.

There are other ways to do this if you're not religious. I suggest keeping a gratitude journal; before going to bed, write down at least three things you're grateful for from that day. It could be something significant, like getting a promotion, or something small, like the moment the morning coffee hit your lips.

When I was in high school, we went inside after lunch each day. The lights were dimmed and the curtains were drawn to create a prayerful state. Then, we spent ten or fifteen minutes in guided prayer that included reflective questions like these:

- When are the moments I am grateful for today?

- What are the small gifts in this day that I might have overlooked?

- Where have I felt joy today?

- When did I give joy to someone?

I carried this practice with me when I went to college. I reflected as I lay down to sleep. I'd get in bed, get comfortable, make the sign of the cross, and think through my day. I do it to this day. I might remember that my wife helped me get out of bed, and I'm grateful for that. Or I remember I was grateful that my brother was home for Mother's Day, and that we sat by the fire, had some drinks, and shared stories. I cherish those moments.

Or maybe we went on a hike and the path was perfectly paved. When that happens, I'm incredibly grateful to be able to be outdoors. Perhaps I was going through the house and heard my family laughing at something, and that simple moment gave me joy. The practice allows me to reflect on the positives of the day, especially the small moments I might have overlooked.

Yes, there are also challenges on any day I reflect on. As I'm writing this book, there was one day recently when I struggled through my workout. All workouts are tough, but this was especially difficult. My body was just not cooperating, and it was mentally painful. It was so difficult that my mom started tearing up as she watched me persevere. I continued to push through even though my body wasn't cooperating because I knew what it meant for the people who followed me and what I would receive from them in return.

As I went through my examen, I didn't reflect on how hard the workout was. I reflected on how grateful I was to be able to walk two hundred yards. I'm not going to dwell on the fact that my mom shed tears. I'm not going to reflect on how I *only* walked two hundred yards, why this happened to me, or why I have this burden. I'm going to be grateful that I was able to get it done.

There's a popular saying that goes, "You don't know what you have until it's gone." I think that's a horrible way to live and a trap we should all work to avoid. Why should we wait to lose something before we start showing appreciation for it?

It's important to keep track of all our blessings, big and small, and use them to make the most of our lives. Using that focus in the examen leaves me feeling grateful and prepares my mindset for the next day, which I know I'm going to start with a review of social media messages. It's all part of the mental diet I follow to control my mindset.

REFLECTION QUESTIONS

1. Do you notice negative patterns in your emotional responses to certain news, media, or relationships? In what ways can you remove or set boundaries with toxic influences that consistently make you feel drained or discouraged?

2. What makes you feel positive and inspired? How can you actively incorporate those things into your daily mental diet?

3. What's something you're grateful for today that you may have overlooked? How can you incorporate more gratitude into your mindset?

Chapter 5
KEEP YOUR SENSE OF HUMOR

A person without a sense of humor is like a wagon without springs. It's jolted by every pebble on the road.

—HENRY WARD BEECHER, *ROYAL TRUTHS*

ONE TIME DR. Peter Venkman examined me. Yes, the famed Ghostbuster with a PhD in parapsychology, better known as comedian Bill Murray, helped in my healing process. He affirmed the idea that while paralysis is no joke, you better find a way to laugh.

About three and a half months into my recovery, I transferred to Craig Hospital in Englewood, Colorado, for rehabilitation. By chance, my mom had left earlier in the day to see my younger brother for his birthday. She had been at my side every day since the moment of my injury until finally taking a little time to go home. My grandparents (my mom's folks) came to stay with me.

That's when Dr. Thomas Balazy, the medical director at Craig Hospital, knocked on the door of my room. He said there was somebody there to see me. I assumed it was a stranger who lived in the area. There had been a number of local visitors who had heard about my story and came to visit me in the last couple of months.

I wheeled my way out of my room and there, in the flesh, was Murray. He stood there in salmon-colored pants, a wrinkled button-down shirt, and a shock of uncombed whitish-gray hair.

I was starstruck. I just kept repeating, "No way! No way! There's no way Bill Murray's standing right in front of me!" It turns out he and Balazy had been roommates for a year at Regis University in Denver when Murray was considering becoming a doctor. Murray had come to Colorado for a reunion.

Murray borrowed Balazy's stethoscope and began to "examine" me. He put it to my head and said he noted that I had some "crazy thoughts in there." He asked me how I got hurt. He talked to me about the future a little bit.

Most importantly, for about six minutes, he reminded me how important laughter and amusement are. It didn't take long for the hallway outside my room to fill up as word got around that Murray was there. What was also pretty cool was that Murray didn't have any photographers or reporters with him. He wasn't doing this for publicity, just out of the goodness of his heart.

Here was this comedy legend from movies like *Ghostbusters*, *Stripes*, *Groundhog Day*, *Caddyshack*, and so many others standing right in front of me, joking around, and trying to brighten my day. That may not be the same as performing surgery like a real doctor, but it's an important part of healing.

It reminded me of what I had worked to do all along: return to being myself.

That's why I'm thankful for that moment, for the time when a muscle spasm became a running gag, and for *Forrest Gump* saving me from the ceiling tiles. I'll get back to those other topics, but let me stress that I understand all too well that whatever physical or mental trauma, addiction, or daunting goal you may face is no laughing matter.

But for your own sake, you need to find humor amid the struggle, even if it's just a chuckle. You must find some light in the darkness, if for no other reason than to regain a sense of normalcy and sanity. Without it, you could easily slip into an abyss of self-pity, anger, and despair. It's also possible to become so serious that you're nearly unapproachable, so consumed by negativity that you're no longer the person you were before.

Worse, you become someone people don't want to be around.

I've seen it. I've heard about it. I've felt the urges myself. Somehow, some way, you have to keep those feelings at bay.

It's part of remaining upbeat, which I had to do from moment one, such as when my brother came to see me for the first time in the hospital. I needed him to be strong and upbeat for me, and vice versa. Likewise, my mom did everything she could to help my friends and family understand and feed my positivity. When visitors came to see me in the hospital, she briefed them on staying upbeat.

My mom wrote about it in the journal she kept. Many of my friends showed up in a somber state. Some of them were crying and visibly depressed. My mom wasn't having it. She looked at my friends and told them to get it together before they saw me. Any type of negativity had to be squashed.

In turn, I had to do my best to be myself. I wasn't Robert "the quadriplegic" or Robert "the guy fighting for his life." It was just me, the guy wanting to hang out with my friends. I was going to be upbeat and strong. I was going to joke around.

Like the time I let one of my friends believe he was a miracle worker.

About two and a half weeks after my injury, I was asleep when my muscles began spasming uncontrollably. Up to that point, my body had been totally limp.

In the middle of that particular night, I awoke and my body seized up. My hips bowed forward, and I could feel the muscles along my spine and lower back contract forcefully. My hamstrings and hip flexors kicked in, pulling my knees up as if I were going into a cannonball. Then my back arched out and I stayed locked in that position.

I was freaked out. I had no idea what was going on. My mom was sitting next to me sleeping. I woke her up and asked her what was happening. She tried to stretch me out to a more comfortable position, but she couldn't do it, so she called a nurse. It was only a little uncomfortable, but I didn't want to sleep through it. I was worried about what the spasms were doing to my muscles. It's also difficult to regain full range of motion if you stay contracted like that for too long.

After that initial episode, I started to get a lot more spasms, and I understood that they were a common symptom of these injuries. I still get them to this day, but they don't freak me out anymore.

Early on, there were spasms like the first one. Then there were spasms when my legs straightened and began shaking violently. I also get spasms in my wrists and hands. They flex up and my fingernails dig into the palms of my hands.

Anyway, this first leg spasm happened and then a few days later some of my teammates came to visit. They didn't know about the spasms, and at one point, one of my teammates touched my leg to get a sense of how much muscle mass I had already lost. As he did, my leg started to shake.

I didn't miss a beat. I started playing it up. I said, "John, I can move again! It's a miracle! You healed me!" For a second, I could see he was confused, like he actually might have had some healing power over me. Then I smiled and explained what was going on.

He looked at me like, "You jerk," and we all burst out laughing.

Then there was this pretty dark line I used with my friend Tyler. As I've mentioned, my goal at Cal was to get into the Haas School of Business undergraduate program. It's hard to do. Only roughly 20 percent of the Cal students who apply get into Haas. And remember that only about 15 percent of people who apply to Cal get in.

When you apply to Haas, it's a combination of your grade point average, résumé, and essay responses. Being an athlete helps, but it's far from a guarantee. One day after the injury when Tyler was visiting, we talked about me applying to Haas. That's when I said, "I'm going to be able to write a hell of an application essay now."

Is that too dark of a sense of humor? It's probably darker than some people can handle. But it's my sense of humor, and it sure makes my friends and me laugh. More than anything, it's me being me. It's me putting my friends at ease about how they talk to me. I didn't want to lose the sense of who I was, and I didn't want them to feel like they had to walk on eggshells around me.

Trust me, my buddies don't cut me much slack anymore, and I love it because it pushes me. Sometimes we'll go into a restaurant and there will be a step up to get inside. While

I'm trying to figure out a way around the step, they'll look at me and say, "Hey, what's the holdup, Paylor?"

After the miracle worker crack, I deserve that.

My family is not spared from my devilish sense of humor. Apart from random visits from comedy legends, Craig Hospital encourages patients to do the activities they did before their injury. Whether it's sailing or scuba diving, the people at Craig Hospital believe in helping patients return to what they love in new, adaptive ways.

That takes some engineering and precautions along the way. You can't just put a paralyzed patient in a kayak, leave them, and say, "Have fun!" I wanted to go fishing again. That was one of my favorite activities with my brother. Our family has a vacation house on Clear Lake in Northern California, which has some of the best bass fishing in the country, if not the world.

When we were younger, I'd wake my brother up and we'd go to the dock. He was a trooper, even though he might be the worst fisherman in the world. As I write this, he has never caught a fish. He is the exception to the proverb that if you teach a man to fish, he will eat for a lifetime.

My brother would starve.

The folks at Craig Hospital made an adaptive pole for me to cast and reel. I still didn't have much use of my hands and arms, but I had enough control to make it work. Plus, there are all sorts of amazing devices that allow completely paralyzed people to fish even if all they can do is breathe.

Anyway, a bunch of us were on the outing doing different activities as I set up by a pond stocked with trout. We stayed for almost four hours. I hadn't caught anything when they announced that we had to start getting ready to leave.

I started casting and reeling as furiously as I could. I desperately wanted to catch a fish. I had a bet with one of my therapists, who is a vegetarian, that if I caught a fish, she had to eat a bite. I had to make this happen.

Finally, I caught one! As a fisherman, I know I should tell you a whopper of a story about how big it was. I can't. This fish was tiny. I could basically cup the fish inside my two hands. It was a glorified sardine.

Still, I took a picture with it. At that moment, all that mattered was I caught a fish. That's when I texted the picture to my brother with the message: "I have officially caught more fish as a quadriplegic than you have in your entire life."

That's brotherly love.

Sidenote: My therapist never had to eat the fish because I caught a cold the next day and couldn't cook it. But I roasted my brother, so it was worth it.

That type of treatment is reserved for me, my family, and my closest friends. It's for that critical inner circle of people you really need to lean on when times get tough.

You have to lift those people up as much as you can. You can't constantly pull them down into your dark feelings. You have to energize them, and laughing is a way of doing that. You need to accept your circumstances and be yourself. It's a challenge. A big one.

Almost like the challenge of being the foremost expert in *Forrest Gump* trivia in the world. That's me. I'm ready to take on anyone when it comes to that movie.

I realize I should probably list a Bill Murray movie as my favorite. He deserves that for his kindness. But Tom

Hanks as Forrest was there for me even before Murray visited. Forrest was there to save me from the ceiling tiles.

I'm talking about those acoustic ceiling tiles you see in large office buildings or, in my case, hospitals. They are those inexpensive, builder-grade, speckled, drop-ceiling tiles that you find at Lowe's, Home Depot, or other hardware stores.

They're intentionally nondescript. They just fade into the background. Nobody ever really looks at those plain ceiling tiles. That is until your neck is in a brace as you recover from a traumatic injury and subsequent surgery that leaves you unable to turn your head.

As you lie on your back, your field of vision is restricted to how far your eyeballs can move from side to side and up and down. Suddenly, your view of the world has become monotonously small.

Aside from recovering from surgery, adjusting to my new life, and fighting off pneumonia, monotony became part of the process. Monotony can feel like torture and drive you crazy. One form of monotony was listening to the monitors attached to my body as they constantly beeped. The room's view was worse.

I had three views depending on how my body was turned to avoid getting a bedsore. I could look at the wall to my left, the monitors on my right, or straight ahead toward a television that hung from the ceiling. If I looked straight up, there were the ceiling tiles.

Those tiles have dots arranged in a seemingly random fashion. If you stare at the tiles long enough, you get caught up in them. I never actually counted all of the dots, but I got close. Worse, I imagined spending minute after minute, hour after hour, and day after day staring at those tiles.

When that happens, life is no longer like a box of chocolates.

Forrest Gump was my solution. The television that hung from the ceiling had a video player attached, but no cable or online access. There were a limited number of movies to watch, and I didn't know most of them. I knew *Forrest Gump*. More specifically, I loved *Forrest Gump*.

I love the tale of a simple, innocent person throwing himself into life with no sense of guile and coming out on the other end happy and successful. It's both heart-warming and motivating. It played on a loop as I lay in that hospital bed. Between checkups, endless pneumonia treatments, and the constant sound of the monitors, watching *Forrest Gump* became my escape.

These days, I'm waiting for Cal to send me a PhD in *Forrest Gump*. I have the test to prove it. I just don't have the pencil.

A little more than a year after my accident, my family and I went on vacation. We ended up going to a Bubba Gump Shrimp Co. restaurant. Before my injury, I had been to the Bubba Gump restaurant in Monterey, California. I noticed they had a *Forrest Gump* trivia contest. The winner got a Bubba Gump pencil or some other trinket.

At that moment on vacation, I was determined to win that pencil. I was looking forward to this trivia game. Yeah, it's silly, but that's kind of the point. If you're going to spend nearly a month watching one movie on an endless loop, you should be ready to win a trivia contest and that Bubba Gump pencil.

I *wanted* that pencil. I *needed* that pencil.

So, the waitress came to the table, and I was geeked up. I was actually more interested in the trivia game than ordering food. My family chuckled at the whole scene as

I grilled the waitress. When is the first question? How many do I have to answer? Do I get better prizes the more questions I get right? Can I work myself all the way up to maybe a keychain, a golf ball, or even, dare I say, a Bubba Gump T-shirt?

I was dreaming big.

The trivia questions started off pretty easy. It was like, what was the name of Forrest's lieutenant when he was in the army? Everybody knows Lieutenant Dan. Then, the questions got a little more specific, such as what is the name of the city where Forrest grew up?

"It's the fictional town of Greenbow, Alabama."

Boom. Bring it on!

I flew through all the questions, and the waitress was a little flabbergasted. She didn't quite know what to do, so she brought over a more experienced waitress to ask me questions. OK, you want to play it that way, huh? I'm thinking I'm on the road to winning every Bubba Gump tchotchke known to man. I'm getting the pencil, the keychain, the golf ball, *and* the T-shirt.

I might even parlay this whole paralyzing injury thing into entering the *Forrest Gump* trivia Hall of Fame, which is just as real as Greenbow.

The second waitress came over and the questions got a little harder. What was the bus number Forrest was waiting for to see Jenny? "Nine." What is Jenny's apartment number? They don't even say it in the movie, you just see it for a second when Forrest knocks on the door.

"Four." C'mon, got anything tough for me?

The second waitress tried me with a question she thought was tough: What was the analogy the doctor used to describe Forrest's back?

"As crooked as a politician."

Seriously, is that the best you've got?

That's when the second waitress decided to get the manager to ask me more questions. Now, I figure they're probably going to offer me a job running the trivia contest or at least a solid gold trophy in recognition of my Gump genius. One way or another, I'm on my way to fame and fortune in the *Forrest Gump* trivia world.

The manager comes over and the questions amp to another level. What was the name of the hurricane that hit the Gulf Coast with Forrest and Lieutenant Dan on board their shrimp boat?

What? Do you think I'm some kind of amateur? "It's Carmen."

Nailed it.

The questions went on and on. I ended up getting two wrong. One was, what was Jenny's address where she grew up in Greenbow. The other was to name the book Forrest brought for his first day of school. I thought it was *Curious George* because that was his favorite book. It was *Big Chief.*

After going through three employees and their questions, I was ready for my prize.

So what happens? No pencil. What do you mean no pencil? Wait a second, how do I not get a pencil? I should be getting a standing ovation from the other patrons. I should be getting equity in Bubba Gump restaurants. This should be the top play on ESPN SportsCenter!

Instead, I couldn't even get a pencil. This is the kind of stuff you have to laugh at.

Then there are some really awkward things, like the time we went to a bar for my twenty-first birthday. I was at Craig Hospital for my birthday in early November, but when I came home for Thanksgiving, a bunch of my friends came over to grab some beers.

We decided to go to a great dive bar in El Dorado Hills. By this point, most people in the area knew me because of all the coverage my injury received. Tyler's mom, who had set up my GoFundMe page, called the bar to let them know I was coming and to make sure my friends and I had a good time. The owner was totally on board.

We got there and they set us up at a table. Everything was going great. Then the manager said to me, "We're going to get you so many drinks that you won't be able to walk out of here!"

She walked away, and my friends and I were staring at each other. Not going to be able to walk out of here? Don't worry, I've got that covered already.

As soon as she left, we all erupted in laughter. It was just hysterical. I know that woman didn't mean to say that, and she may not have even realized what she said. It was just a faux pas. We've all done that, but it sure was funny.

Of course, some people in my position might have been offended by that comment. Not me. It's just one of those harmless things that people say without thinking. I'm not going to hold it against her. I'm just going to laugh.

It's like when people stare at me. It happens all the time, especially with little kids. I was at Bass Pro Shops one time and this four- or five-year-old kid was staring at me. He had probably never seen anybody in a wheelchair before. The funny part is that he was staring at me while walking and stopped paying attention to what was in front of him. After a few steps, he ran straight into a table and tumbled onto his back. He wasn't hurt at all, so I couldn't help but laugh.

I also get lots of little kids who come up and ask me, "Why can't you walk?" I explain it to them, and they usually ask a couple more questions before they leave. Once in a while, however, they ask that same question over and over again. They might alternate a different question in between each time they repeat, "Why can't you walk?"

If they ask enough times, sometimes I will say, "Because I didn't eat my vegetables."

Parents owe me some gratitude for that.

Reflection Questions

1. Who are the people in your life that can make you laugh and with whom you can be yourself?

2. Can you recall a time when humor helped you deflect negativity and maintain a positive outlook? What helped you find humor in the moment?

3. When was the last time you found yourself laughing, even for a moment? What sparked that?

Chapter 6

MAKE A COMMITMENT TO OTHERS

I don't know if we each have a destiny, or if we're all just
floatin' around accidental-like on a breeze, but I think maybe
it's both. Maybe both happenin' at the same time.

—FORREST GUMP

THIS IS THE story of Talon Bonanno.
When Talon was about fourteen years old, he
came to compete in the summer youth rugby camp
at Jesuit High School. Talon was small. Really small.
Maybe five feet tall and around eighty pounds.

He loved rugby, and his passion was clear, but there's a
point where size matters in certain sports. You can love
basketball all you want, but you're probably not going to
play at a high level if you're not tall enough. In rugby, a
certain degree of size and strength is a prerequisite.

For Talon, rugby wasn't so much about being the best
player as it was about wanting to break out of his shell.
When he arrived at camp, he was shy and a little intimi-
dated. I had just finished my freshman year at Cal and
returned to serve as a coach. So, I made it my job to help
him accomplish the most basic thing he wanted to do: be
part of the group.

During practices, I gave Talon the ball, scooped him

up, and carried him through the crowd of players until he scored. He ate it up and had a giant grin on his face. It made him so happy. We did it plenty of times.

After practice, Talon would tell his mom all about it.

"When I picked up Talon that day when Robert first did that, Talon was so excited about what had happened," Christine Bonanno, Talon's mother, said. "Talon said Coach Robert had made him feel so important and a part of the whole process. From that day on, all Talon wanted to do was go to Jesuit High and play rugby for the school just like Robert. He never could play rugby because he was always too small...but that time made him so happy."

This is the essence of making a selfless commitment.

Whether we realize it or not, we're all committed to something. In each goal we strive to accomplish, there's someone who we are looking to benefit, whether that be ourselves or others.

I know I've talked about preparation on a personal level and how giving my best effort paid off in building a foundation that survived the trauma of my injury. There's also the boost my mental diet gets when I read the messages of those I've inspired.

But there's another step in this process that goes beyond preparation and feeding off the encouragement you get from people. It's the mission you enter through a selfless commitment to others. It's understanding the purpose-based motivation that comes from serving others, and how that form of motivation pushes us further than selfish desires.

I come from a family where I had a privileged upbringing. I know that and I'm grateful for it. At the same time, my family built the expectation that I would give back. Talon was a small example of that, and I'll get back to his story in a moment.

From the time I started school, life was about serving others. I remember making peanut butter and jelly sandwiches for the homeless when I was in kindergarten. Later on, we would all sit down and write Christmas cards during the holidays for soldiers who were fighting overseas and couldn't be with their families.

As I got older, our community service became more hands-on, such as volunteering at homeless shelters and running clothing drives at school. You become committed to making a positive difference in other people's lives when you see the impact it makes

At Jesuit, the motto is "Men for Others." By my senior year, we were required to perform fifty hours of community service. We could either accomplish it alone or participate in what was called an immersion. In the immersion program, we spent a week in an impoverished community helping the people who lived there.

I had the privilege of going to the Blackfeet Indian Reservation for my immersion. It's way up on the northern side of Montana and borders Canada, just east of Glacier National Park.

It's a beautiful part of the country and mostly untouched by humans. It's also very poor. When I was there, it was downtrodden. You're talking about a group of incredibly isolated people, so developing an industry for jobs and an economy is tough. Not to mention the fallout the Blackfeet Tribe continues to endure after its battles with the US government.

At one point, the tribe had an unemployment rate of 69 percent. Of those who worked, 26 percent of them earned below the poverty line. As a result, you have some very basic problems, such as how to deal with garbage. Who is going to haul trash away if you don't have money to pay for it?

Trash was scattered all over the tribal property. It collected on the sides of fences and buildings, sometimes forming piles up to five feet high. When you live in that type of environment, it's hard for people to stay healthy or have a positive quality of life. We're talking about a lack of basic things that so many of us take for granted.

Aside from collecting trash, we did whatever the community asked of us. We built fences for the elderly. We went to the local elementary school and tutored the kids in math and reading. One time, we played sports with the kids. They loved me because I could dunk a basketball. We also put together some marketing material for a powwow they were having.

We did anything we could to make a difference, and they were so appreciative. It was one of those times when I felt like there was no end to what we could do. Every night, the eight of us from Jesuit would do a reflection on what we had seen and accomplished that day.

All of this was about serving other people and the mission we were on to help this marginalized community. When you do that, you build a sense of purpose in your life.

Yes, I had personal goals at the time, and I still do, even if they have changed. I wanted to be a great rugby player and go to Cal. And when I became paralyzed, I had the selfish desire to regain mobility just for my own satisfaction and quality of life. My commitment was to myself and for myself.

The word *selfish* usually has a negative connotation, but my selfish desire wasn't necessarily negative. Who could blame me for wanting to walk and live a normal life for my own pleasure? An outlook like that is expected for anyone in a situation like mine.

But my commitment to others forever changed six days into my injury.

As I dealt with the medical complications of pneumonia, an inability to swallow, and the mental trauma of being unable to move, Jesuit High School hosted a service to pray for my healing and fortitude.

On that same day, my dad showed me a Facebook post of a kid I didn't recognize. He was pale, incredibly skinny, and had sparse white hair. It was clear this kid was fighting for his life.

It was Talon.

By March 2017, Talon was attending Jesuit, and he was hit with devastating news. Just two months before I got hurt, doctors discovered that Talon had a rare form of cancer called neuroblastoma in one of his kidneys. It was stage 4. He quickly ended up in the Kaiser Permanente Roseville Women & Children's Center in California for treatment.

In the Facebook post, Talon's mom wrote a caption along with the picture, and my dad read it aloud.

> Today Talon is spending another day at (the hospital) getting blood. Yesterday he received 2 units of platelets and had an allergic reaction…hives. They took care of him quickly, but it was pretty scary for Talon and myself. So please pray today no reactions!!
>
> We wanted to attend the Mass for Robert Paylor at Jesuit this morning, but had to be here. Talon wanted to show his support for Robert, so he is wearing his rugby shirt that Jesuit gifted him while he was getting his first round of chemo. Robert

was one of Talon's inspirations for wanting to play rugby. After attending a few of the rugby camps at Jesuit during the summers, he would always come home laughing and smiling. Telling us how Robert would grab him and run all the way to make a score because he was smaller than most of the players. And what a nice person he was. It lit up Talon's day!

Talon's goal when he is all cured and strong again is that he will be playing rugby for Jesuit and we have faith that is happening!

We are praying for your healing and a quick recovery. Be strong and keep smiling...your strength helps Talon stay strong too!

As I listened to those words, I wept. I had received more notes of support than I could even read, and I appreciated every one of them. But the message from Talon's mom transformed my life and is etched into my soul. It made me understand why a commitment to others was so important. It made me realize that taking on my challenge was not about me.

My commitment forever changed as my dad read the post. I vowed that I would fight as long as it takes and with everything I have. I would do it for Talon and for all of those who are inspired by this journey.

I found my purpose.

Selfish desires can be motivating, but in my experience, they don't provide the sense of purpose that is required to overcome life's greatest challenges. To overcome true adversity or achieve ambitious goals, our commitment must extend beyond ourselves. To cultivate a sense of purpose, we need a reason to persevere beyond our individual gain.

If my rehabilitation were just about my self-interest, I'm

confident I wouldn't be giving the same effort as I do each day and have given the last eight years. The selfish desire to walk and regain a functioning body hasn't fueled my fight against this challenge.

My rehab is painful. Not physically painful, but mentally draining. By the end of each workout, my body is exhausted, and every step demands my full effort. I grit my teeth, squint my eyes, and grunt just to place one of my feet inches in front of the other. Struggling so intensely just for the pleasure of walking a few laps around my house doesn't motivate me to get up the next day and do it again.

Beyond that, the slow and inconsistent nature of my progress can be aggravating. I've fought this battle for more than eight years and I still use a wheelchair every day. In the vast majority of my workouts, I'm not setting new personal bests or making noticeable improvements. I press on week after week and then I see a small bump of improvement. For every day of growth, there are about thirty stagnant days.

Still, I get up every day and fight because of my commitment to others. I have to give my full effort in my workouts. I have to share a daily post of me taking on my challenge. People are counting on me. My posts inspire them to overcome their hardships and accomplish their goals. Those posts might help them continue to press forward when they feel like giving up.

This is the biggest commitment I have ever made, so I can't quit. I need to keep fighting for others. That has sustained me all these days.

There were also others who helped form my selfless commitment. One special person I have never even met touched my heart. My dad's friend's mother was approaching the end of her life. Her name was Joyce Zuidema. During her final days, family members and close friends visited to say their goodbyes.

Instead of speaking with them, she heard about my story and started praying for me. Though I'd never met her and shared only a distant connection, she dedicated her final days to praying for me. Think about that.

Her daughter told my dad that people would come to her door to visit, and she would say, "I'm sorry, I appreciate you visiting, but I don't have time to talk. I'm praying for Robert." Another story I was told is that she said, "Tell Robert I'll be waiting for him at the gates of heaven." She died on May 18, only twelve days after I was injured. I was flabbergasted, completely blown away by the love this woman showed me as she faced death.

I just thought about how utterly incredible it is for someone to think of me while suffering so much. That's a true commitment to something beyond yourself. I'm both grateful and humbled.

Another example was Don Brophy, grandfather to two of my Cal teammates, Nick and Anthony Salaber. Like Zuidema, Don was in the final days of his life and prayed for me as well. He died on June 24, 2017, and requested that anyone making a donation in his honor contribute to my GoFundMe rehabilitation fund.

These individuals, alongside Talon and his family, showed me my purpose: to live for others. It shows the impact one can have on someone's life by choosing to persevere.

My dream of being an athlete is gone, but my ability to move people is not. Of course, Talon ended up needing far more than I could ever provide. He grew to about five foot six and still never weighed much more than about eighty pounds. There were signs that he should have been much bigger, such as his size twelve feet. The cancer inhibited his ability to grow.

But the cancer couldn't inhibit his spirit.

I'll let his mother tell the rest of the story.

Eventually, Talon was cancer-free for a year and a half before he had a relapse, and the cancer was in his spine. He eventually couldn't walk, and the doctors told him he was never going to walk again.

But he did eventually walk. He would watch Robert's videos every day, over and over again. He'd tell me sometimes, "Play it again." Or I'd see him sitting on the couch and a lot of the time he'd be watching television, or he'd be on his tablet and I'd ask, "What are you watching?" and he'd say he was watching one of Robert's videos.

I really don't know how he did it, but he walked. He would make it across the house. It wasn't far and it was a struggle, but he did it and that was important to him. He and Robert both have this fighter's spirit. That's what I think it is about both of them. They just fight.

I told Talon a bunch of times that I just wouldn't be able to do that. I don't have that kind of fight. I would have just given up. It would have been too hard for me, but those two had this special bond that way.

He said that Coach Robert had made him feel so important and a part of the whole process. From that day on, all Talon wanted to do was go to Jesuit and play rugby for the school just like Robert. He never could play rugby because he was always too small and then he got sick, but that time made him so happy.

So, when we heard that Robert had gotten hurt

and Talon couldn't be there, he just wanted to pray for Robert. Talon died Jan. 25, 2021. He didn't die from the cancer. It was the impact the radiation treatments had on his lungs when they tried to treat the cancer in his spine.

Talon had the most faith and belief of any human being I have ever met. Right up until the end, he believed he was going to get better.

I was thinking about that week at camp. I really believe God had a plan with the two of them that long ago. There's a reason that they met.

I know there was a reason with every fiber of my being.

Talon embodies what it means to live with a selfless commitment more than anyone I know, and I will spend the rest of my life sharing the example he left on how we ought to live.

Here was someone who had every reason to complain and feel sorry for himself. He shouldn't have had to spend years in and out of hospitals battling illness and fatigue. He should've been in high school with his friends, playing sports, and building a foundation that he would take into a long life.

But when my high school hosted that prayer service a few days after my injury, he wasn't thinking about himself. He was thinking about me. While he was battling stage 4 cancer, he was praying for me. His ability to look beyond himself is astonishing to me and is an example I aspire to live up to.

Talon's life on earth ended far too early, but his spirit lives on in me and so many others that we will try to live as he did—selflessly. He is my role model and the most inspirational person I have ever met.

That's why a commitment is so important. It gets us out

of bed in the morning and it helps us put in extra hours when we feel like slowing down. A commitment can motivate the crippled to walk and give peace to the sick. When adversity strikes and we're struggling to find a reason to keep moving forward, our commitment to others is our reason.

So, ask yourself, "Who is my commitment to?" Is it your family? A friend? Your coworkers? Is it maybe someone you don't even personally know? Visualize their faces, what they're going through, and how you can make their life better.

Now make that commitment like an unbreakable contract, and let it guide all of your actions and thoughts.

A life lived for others is a life of purpose. And purpose is what powers us through our challenges.

Reflection questions

1. Who are the people you care most about in your life, and how can you make a positive impact on them?

2. How would your life look different if you dedicated your time, energy, and skills not for yourself but for the betterment of others?

3. Who has supported you during tough times, and what did that support mean to you? How can you pay it forward to someone else in a similar way?

Chapter 7

DON'T DELAY HAPPINESS

Life moves pretty fast. If you don't stop and look
around once in a while, you could miss it.

—FERRIS BUELLER

I SHED TEARS AT a Darius Rucker concert.
I realize I'm going to get some crap from my buddies for admitting that. Fair enough, I would do the
same to them if the roles were reversed. In my defense, it
wasn't entirely Rucker's music that got me teary-eyed. It
was the setting and a moment that caused me to rethink
my journey.

And it was Rucker's music that helped me see my life
differently.

I was at the Red Rocks Amphitheatre outside of Denver,
one of the most beautiful concert venues in the world. I
was listening to Rucker belt out his brand of country
music surrounded by people who were dancing, laughing,
and singing along.

I had just survived my near-death injury. By all rights,
this should have been a moment to enjoy, one of my first
real opportunities to return to a sense of normalcy. Instead,
it was hard not to think about what I wasn't able to do. I
couldn't dance or sway to the music the way other people

were. Those thoughts were tainting what should have been a perfect moment. Then, I furthered my resolve to walk again.

None of that reaction was altogether healthy.

It was an important part of learning this lesson: don't delay your happiness waiting for a great achievement that you think will change your life.

You can tie that up in some other cliché if you like. You can stop and smell the roses. You can enjoy the little things in life before you realize they are the big things. You can savor the sunshine while it lasts.

All are variations on the theme I'm explaining. I spent the better part of a year waiting for some great, triumphant moment in my recovery. When that moment finally happened, it was surprisingly underwhelming, more like checking off a to-do list than a grand celebration.

Along the way, it would have been easy to let the moments to enjoy life pass me by. I sat at Red Rocks, listening to one of my favorite musicians, and the thoughts of what I didn't have were swimming in my head, instead of fully living in that moment.

Before we get to the concert, let's rewind to the first month after my injury. I was at Santa Clara Valley Medical Center, which was a blessing in so many ways. It's one of the best hospitals in the country for spinal cord injuries. My survival is proof of that reputation. The people there literally saved my life. That's a debt I can never repay and for which I will always be grateful.

When it comes to rehabilitation, however, I needed a different approach. Here I was, twenty years old and a highly trained athlete who had a combination of both mental strength and endurance to compete at a national championship level.

I was not the typical patient. I wanted to be hyperaggressive. Moreover, recovering from a spinal cord injury demands aggression. What doctors explained is that optimal healing and recovery occur in the early period after an injury.

The more effort you put into your recovery early on, the greater the potential payoff in the long run. As an athlete, when I hear that instruction, all I say is, "Let's go!" The first time I went into a weight room with the physical therapists at Santa Clara Valley Medical Center, I did different weightlifting exercises to see what I could handle. I wanted to push myself right from the start. I wasn't lifting much weight at all, but I was giving all the effort I had like I did back in the weight room at Cal.

Functionally, I literally couldn't break a sweat, no matter how much I wanted to. One of the lesser-known symptoms of spinal cord injuries is the inability to regulate body temperature. I had to be careful not to overheat.

The physical therapists saw me and immediately told me to back off, put the weight down, and take it easy. They said I was pushing my heart rate too high. I thought, "Pushing my heart rate too high? Isn't that exactly what a workout is supposed to do?"

I had therapy for about three hours a day. One hour of physical therapy, one hour of occupational therapy, and then one hour of weight training. I would go to a couple of educational classes, then maybe meet with some visitors and see friends. In my view, I wasn't fully dedicated to overcoming this injury. If I was going to conquer the odds, I needed to entirely throw myself into rehab.

The other issue was that my biggest outing at the Santa Clara hospital was to go to Cold Stone Creamery for dessert. The ice cream was great, and it was nice to get out, but the idea that this was one of the biggest excursions for getting "back to normal" wasn't enough. To me, there had to be more to look forward to in life, even if that life looked different than before.

Ultimately, I was locked in a mental tug-of-war with the staff at Santa Clara. Every day, we would go to the gym to work out for an hour. I would push myself, and the spike in my blood pressure and heart rate monitors would instantly put the therapists on high alert.

Right around this time, my family and I heard from the family of Jake Javier, who was paralyzed in June 2016 after diving into a swimming pool the day before his high school graduation. Javier was extremely active. He had been a football player at San Ramon Valley High and was planning to play in college.

Like me, he started at Santa Clara Valley Medical Center and wanted to be more aggressive with his rehab. His family eventually found Craig Hospital in Englewood, Colorado, the suburbs of Denver. His family highly recommended it to my family and me.

As soon as I saw the information, I was sold. The majestic views of the Rocky Mountains on the website were a great starting point. More importantly, the perspective on rehabilitation was key. In so many words, the philosophy at Craig Hospital was, "Whatever you think you can handle, we'll give it to you." Additionally, the philosophy there was to push patients to get back to as much of their previous lives as possible in new, adaptive ways.

If that meant scuba diving for a quadriplegic, the administration there was going to try to find a way. If that meant fishing for someone who can't move their arms, they were still going to take them fishing. The goal was to maximize every patient's recovery, whatever that meant.

In my mind, that meant I was going to walk again. I already had a vision that when I returned to Cal, I was going to walk triumphantly through campus. The prospect of going to Craig fueled that dream. Where I sometimes let it get astray was when I attached my happiness to it. Essentially, I couldn't be truly satisfied or happy until I reached my goal.

That type of approach can leave you sulking at a concert when you should be enjoying yourself. Worse, it can leave you underwhelmed when you do reach a major goal.

As I sat through that concert, a lot of my thinking was wrapped up in the emotional intensity of what I was dealing with. Surviving this injury was the greatest challenge of my life and probably will be when it's all said and done.

But there was also the mental challenge. As we say in the sports world, the enemy of great is good. The notion is that when you become good at something, you become satisfied, which leads to complacency and ultimately stops you from becoming great.

So, as I prepared to go to Craig Hospital, I was fixated on chasing this lofty goal and knew I wouldn't let up. All the pain and negativity in my life would be washed away once I could stand up and walk. If I just kept my head down early on, I would be satisfied once I got on my feet.

I think you probably know where that ends up, but I'll get back to the point in a minute.

Just *wanting* to go to Craig Hospital wasn't going to make it happen. I had to be accepted first. This was when it became go-time for my dad. While my mom was by my side at every moment in the hospital room, my dad was doing the paperwork and working the phones, which was no easy task. He dealt with red tape and rejection from the insurance companies to get me where I needed to be. It took every bit of his ceaseless energy as a salesman not to get beaten down.

The process was further complicated by Santa Clara Valley Medical Center's high reputation. Beyond that, Santa Clara is a public hospital and Craig Hospital is a private hospital. The insurance companies asked my dad, "Why does your son need a private hospital in Colorado when he's already at one of the best public hospitals for spinal cord injuries?" My dad battled and battled until the insurers finally agreed to cover their share of my care in Colorado.

I flew to Colorado on a private medical transport jet, which was a first for me. Not that it really mattered. I was lying on my back strapped to a gurney the whole time, so I was far from sipping champagne at 30,000 feet.

It was still pretty cool. Who doesn't think being on a private jet is cool?

I got to Craig Hospital, and I immediately went through a series of examinations. The first thing they pointed out was a skin sore on my tailbone. Not good. It must have happened during the trip to Colorado. Again, skin sores are extremely dangerous for quadriplegics, and the tail-bone is one of the worst spots because you sit right on it. I was immediately put on bed rest.

Next, I was evaluated on what is known as the American Spinal Cord Injury Association Impairment Scale, or ASIA scale, for short. The scale goes from level A (complete impairment) to level E (no impairment). The scale is subject to interpretation, so there's some leeway in the process.

The goal is obviously to get as close to level E as you can, and the closer you are from the start of your injury, the better chance you have long term. At Santa Clara, I was measured at level C, which gave me some additional hope that I would one day get close to E. One way they determine if you can move from level B to C is by testing the muscle control in your rectum, as it's at the lowest point of your spinal cord.

Unfortunately, the experts at Craig Hospital said that what was perceived as muscle control was more of a spasm. I was downgraded to level B. That was another gut punch.

Then they started checking the range of motion in my hips and knees. They determined I had something known as heterotopic ossification. That's where your body starts developing bone in soft tissue areas of your joints. It happens to a lot of younger, athletic people who suddenly become completely sedentary. If left untreated, it would completely lock up my hips and knees to where I couldn't move.

Finally, they discovered a blood clot in a major artery leading to my heart. I had to get two injections in my stomach every day. More gut shots, this time literally. I had been there maybe a couple of days, and I couldn't help but think, "What the heck happened? I came here to work out and get on my journey toward walking again, but the first thing that happens is that I take a left hook to the jaw and I'm down on the mat."

And just to add a little dreariness, my first room at the hospital had a view of a brick wall. Instead of the majestic Rockies, I got bricks. I came all the way to Colorado, got hit with a grand slam of maladies, and didn't get to see the mountains. It was so bad that all I could do was laugh. It took a few days and some prodding from my mom, but I finally got a different room.

Really, the rough start was more promising than

perturbing. This was an indication of the type of care I was going to get throughout my time at Craig Hospital. The intense attention to detail made all the difference.

Then came the best part. I met with the people who were going to take care of me over the coming months. I met with them individually and then as a team. There was the primary doctor in charge of my care, the primary nurse, the physical therapist, the occupational therapist, the speech therapist, the psychiatrist, and the recreational therapist.

This was more in line with what I was used to as an athlete. There was communication and a shared sense of how to achieve the ultimate goal.

Most of all, I needed to hear the speech I got from my doctor, Dr. Johansen, that day. Remember, I had just come from a traumatic, life-threatening situation where the first doctor told me I'd be lucky to lift a piece of pizza. That was followed by a nurse who feared I might die from pneumonia and then by therapists who were trying to get me to back down from working out so hard.

Dr. Johansen immediately restored my hope:

> Robert, what happened to you was terrible, but we don't know where you're going to progress from here. I could tell you that you'll never walk again, and I could be absolutely wrong. I have been wrong too many times to say that I know what's going to happen. I could also tell you that you'll walk out of these doors, but I can also be wrong about that. What I can tell you is that we're going to give you every advantage that modern medicine has to offer. So, if you want to put in the extra hours, we will give you the extra hours. We will give you everything that you can handle. And we're going to have

a team-based approach. You have the full strength
and support of this team.

That was music to my ears as I set about reclaiming my
life. As much as I loved the view of the Rockies, I wasn't
here for a vacation. It was time to get to work, and my
team at Craig was ready to provide.

My schedule was packed with eight to nine hours
of rehabilitation and educational classes a day. I had to
relearn nearly everything, starting with small goals like
being able to put on a shirt, brush my teeth, or push a
manual wheelchair down the hall. We focused on recon-
necting my nervous system and strengthening my body,
using cutting-edge technology that sent electrical pulses
to stimulate muscle contractions. As it worked, I concen-
trated on flexing those muscles on my own, bridging the
gap between my body and my mind.

On weekends, I spent extra time in the gym, practicing
the techniques I'd learned. Was it sometimes frustrating to
struggle with such basic tasks? Of course. But if I wanted
my vision of walking again to become reality, these milestones had to be conquered. Quitting wasn't an option. So,
I gave each session everything I had.

After about a month at Craig, my body began to
respond. I continued my mental exercises, envisioning my
body moving, doing twenty reps per muscle group from
head to toe. Then one day, it happened—a flicker in my
finger, a twitch in my hamstring. The smallest movements,
but it overwhelmed me with emotion. I cried, filled with
hope that all this hard work was starting to pay off.

I shared the developments with my therapists, and they
pushed my rehab to the next level. They said, "This is
amazing! Now we can get you standing and walking!"

I was thinking, "Wait a minute. I just twitched my hamstring, and you're talking about walking?" But that's where their genius and resources shined.

They harnessed me to a winch suspended from the ceiling, lifting me over a treadmill while they manually moved my legs in a walking pattern. They strapped robotic machinery around my legs, guiding me through assisted steps for hours. And as the weeks went on, more muscles woke up. I grew stronger. My vision was starting to materialize.

There was a time when I would've given almost anything just to have the *chance* to walk and move my hands again. Now that single-minded focus fueled me. I wouldn't be distracted by anything until I took those first unassisted steps. That was where I'd find my happiness.

That's where I missed the bigger picture. Or, in the case of Rucker, I didn't enjoy the music the way I should have.

After I got to Denver in June, I met Dan Lyle, who is one of the greatest American rugby players ever. He worked as an executive at the Anschutz Entertainment Group, which operates Red Rocks Amphitheater.

When I was talking to Lyle, I mentioned that Rucker was playing on August 1, 2017, and I told him that I'd love to see that concert. Without hesitation, Lyle said, "Done. You've got tickets." He took care of it, and my mom, my recreational therapist, her fiancé, and I sat in the front row with this amazing view of Rucker as he played. It was going to be awesome.

On top of that, Red Rocks is like a cathedral carved into the base of the mountains. Giant pillars of red rock jut from the foothills, creating an incredible stage, while massive slabs of rock on either side amplify the sound, carrying it perfectly through the open-air environment.

Adding to the ambiance was the breathtaking view of downtown Denver, which only got better as night fell.

People first started playing concerts there in 1906, and Red Rocks officially opened in 1941. It's the type of place people visit even when there's no concert. It's that breathtaking. Some of the greatest acts in music have made their pilgrimage to the venue. U2 recorded its famous concert film *Under a Blood Red Sky* at Red Rocks. Everybody from the Beatles to Bruce Springsteen has played there.

So, here was my moment to take in Rucker at this truly great venue. It was perfect as we sat in the wheelchair-accessible section in the front row. I was barely three months into my rehab and only two months into being at Craig Hospital, so getting out like this was a big deal.

It was an awesome show. As I looked around, people were standing, singing along, and dancing. That's when it hit me—I couldn't stand or dance, and I might never be able to again.

Then, the sadness hit.

This was one of those down moments I had to deal with. I got caught thinking about what I didn't have and what was taken from me. That feeling was normal and expected, but it overwhelmed me. The question was, what was I going to do about it?

At that moment, the answer came in a song by Rucker called "It Won't Be Like This for Long." The song tells the story of a man coping with the travails of being a young father. Whether it's trying to get his daughter to fall asleep when she's young or dealing with her teenage angst, the message is that those are just passing phases. That frustration will come and go, and one day we'll look back on those challenging times and miss them.

Through his lyrics, Rucker reassured me that everything

would be all right. I might have been suffering at that moment, but it would pass. While there were many things to complain about, there were even more to be grateful for.

I listened to those words, and I cried.

Think about it. I had almost died three months before. It felt like I was telling myself, "Come on, Paylor, get your perspective back." I was working with some of the top specialists on paralysis who believed in me and were dedicated to helping me improve. I had my mom by my side, and so many people around the world giving me their love and support.

Yes, certain parts of life had become extremely difficult. You could even go so far as to say they sucked. But as I preach all the time, I had to keep perspective. I was twenty years old and still possessed a lifetime of possibility in front of me. I should have been whooping it up the whole time I was listening to Rucker, not sad because my life had changed. I let that chance to be happy at that moment get away.

Tears wouldn't make me work harder. That's just self-pity, and I'm not about that. A stronger longing wasn't going to make me more intense; I already had that covered. Conversely, happiness wasn't going to make me complacent. I was going to wake up the next day still wanting to walk.

I wasn't going to give up on my goal, leave Craig Hospital, and return home if I had a good night out. In fact, a good night of laughing and singing along might be better for me in the long run. What I do know is that life can change in a moment, and you shouldn't waste the opportunities to be happy.

Most of you will never have to experience what I have gone through, and I sincerely hope you don't. But all of you will have something that you want to achieve, some goal that is difficult and bold. It may consume your focus and that's OK. But don't let it consume your life and the chance to enjoy what's around you.

To put it bluntly, don't go to a concert and dwell on what disappoints you. This was the first lesson in a process that was going to take time to sink in as I stayed focused on my goal.

I spent eleven months at Craig Hospital, and I worked with every bit of intensity I could muster to establish a new pattern for my life. The way I see it, the people at Santa Clara Valley Medical Center saved my life, and the people at Craig Hospital got it back on track. You can't ask for more than that.

I wish I could thank every individual at Craig who played a part in my recovery, but there wouldn't be enough ink to write all their names. They transformed the trajectory of my life in ways I can never fully repay. They know who they are, and they know I am forever grateful.

My time at Craig Hospital was fantastic and exactly what I needed to feed my physical and mental approach. To stay positive, there's a little trick I picked up while I was there that I still use to this day. Initially, it was a way of changing my perspective. Now, it is part of maintaining a positive perspective on what I go through.

I count the days since my injury. It's not unlike people who are recovering from addiction or a traumatic situation. If you have ever seen one of my various social media posts or an interview with me, you have seen me talk about the number of days I have been in my recovery since my accident. Whether that's day 300 or day 2,300, I make sure to note it.

It's part of what many people like to call "stacking the

days." Not every day in my life has a monumental achievement, like graduating from college, taking my first steps,
or setting a new personal best in my rehab. As I've said,
the vast majority of my days don't show any noticeable
improvement.

At the same time, every day is an achievement.
Achieving a bold goal is like building a skyscraper brick
by brick. Each day I work at it is another intentional step
toward my goal being accomplished. Even if it seems like
another ordinary day, I'm going to be grateful for it, share
it with others, and count it as a capitalized opportunity to
improve. That point of view is a lot healthier than what
crept into my initial perspective.

My frame of mind when I first got to Craig Hospital
was, "I've been at this for thirty days, when is it going
to end?" If I had kept that perspective, I could see how I
might have given in to defeat somewhere along the way.
Again, there is no guarantee that my battle to walk again
is ever going to end.

That was when I started listening to other patients count
the days they had been in rehab. It was like a badge of
honor. The more days they had, the greater their sense of
pride. Every day of rehab was, in and of itself, an achievement on the way to chasing the greater goal. It shifted the
challenge away from endless monotony.

That made perfect sense to me. It aligned with the
intentional and purposeful life I strive to lead. Many days,
it's easy to go through the motions and lose sight of what
you're working toward. When you realize how much effort
you've put in, it starts to feed on itself. You move from
day thirty to day fifty and then on to day one hundred.
Eventually, the days add up to where you're never going
to let up.

As the days add up to the thousands, I'll never quit. Time doesn't have to break us down. It can make us stronger, especially when we learn from the past.

From the day I was injured, I was certain that taking my first steps would change my life. Every day I dreamed of getting on my feet and moving my legs forward, even if it was just an inch. I would lie back at night in tears, imagining what that accomplishment would feel like.

When you lose your ability to walk, you want nothing more than to get it back. I would've given anything but my faith, family, and friends to have that back. I thought taking my first steps would be the largest dopamine rush known to man. That would be a high that would last a lifetime.

After 226 days of fighting, I had finally built up the strength and courage to take my first steps without a harness. Through the endless dedication of my therapists and months of grueling effort, I went from no motion below my chest to being able to twitch my fingers and toes to being prepared to enjoy the victory of taking my first post-injury steps.

On December 18, 2017, I did it. I was in the hospital gym, walking along the basketball court using my walker. My close friend Tyler Douglas stood in front of me and three staff members to the left, right, and behind me. That included physical therapist Eric Vande Griend, who kept my feet steady as I moved them on my own. My mom helped record the video so we could post it to my GoFundMe page.

I cautiously moved my left foot forward, waiting for the rush of dopamine to flood my brain. I moved a few inches, and made a stride with my right foot, again anticipating the rush. I repeated the process until I had walked down and back the basketball court. When I was done, I returned to the side of the gym, sat back in my wheelchair, did a couple of fist bumps and high-fives, and rolled to my next workout. I thought, "Wait, that's it?"

There was no dopamine coursing through my body. There were no fireworks. There was no parade. There was no standing ovation.

I was happy, but it didn't measure up to even a lot of normal life events. Honestly, I got a bigger rush when I got an A on an exam. I felt good about what had just happened, but it wasn't that one moment that was going to change the course of my life the way I had built it up in my head.

I don't even remember what we did to celebrate. We might have gone to Chili's for dinner, which is cool. I love Chili's. In the weeks leading up to those steps, you'd think this would have been the time to head to Morton's, Del Frisco's, or Ruth's Chris Steak House. But when it comes down to it, I just can't say no to bottomless chips and salsa.

The point is, I had waited for this moment, putting off my happiness for months until it happened. As it turned out, it was like a good day at the office. That's why I say, don't suffer today so you can be happy in a month, a year, or whatever it may be. Lift your head up and appreciate what you have now. Goals become destructive when they blind you from seeing your blessings.

It's important to strive for a better life, but not at the cost of overlooking all you currently have. Set audacious goals and build an appetite to make your vision a reality, but don't get so lost in the future that you miss what's right in front of you. At the same time, don't be so focused on soaking up all you currently have that you become complacent. Ambition and gratitude must be in balance. For me, I had to learn how to tone down my constant longing to fully recover.

I can't imagine what my life would look like if I only predicated my happiness on achieving my goal of never needing a wheelchair again. I could spend years, decades, or possibly my entire life focused on one thing I didn't have, unable to see all that I retained and gained. Learning this lesson early on saved me from a life of discontent, and it's a lesson I'll never forget.

My injury taught me that each day is a precious gift, and we should treat each day just like that—a gift. Embrace each day with gratitude. Don't fall into the trap of putting off happiness.

REFLECTION QUESTIONS

1. Are there areas of your life where you might be waiting for a "perfect moment" to enjoy life?

2. In what ways do you find joy in the simple moments and in the things you already have?

3. When you look back on the goals you've worked toward, how many of those moments were as fulfilling as you anticipated? Did you find yourself truly content in those moments, or did you move on to the next task?

Chapter 8
COMPARED TO WHAT?

Robert was silently crying when I woke today. He said he needed me
to help him suction his sinuses. While I did, he told me he awakens
in tears many days. I can't imagine the inner pain he goes through
daily, uncertain of his outcome, his life changed from youthful
exuberance and zest for outdoor living to confinement.

—From the diary of Debbie Paylor, my mom

Y ONE-YEAR ANNIVERSARY of being paralyzed
featured a miracle.

Maybe not the one I wanted, but the one I
needed.

I was coming toward the end of my time at Craig
Hospital in May 2018 when I received an intriguing invitation. The Order of Malta, one of the oldest orders in the
Catholic Church, extended an opportunity for me to go to
Lourdes, France, to bathe in its waters in search of a miracle. Over the past 160 years, an estimated two hundred
million people have visited Lourdes in search of healing.
To date, there is a list of seventy-one recognized miracles
of healing the sick or injured.

Not great odds for me, I understand. In addition, the
Catholic Church's protocols for recognizing an unex-
plained healing as a miracle are highly rigorous. It's a

process that takes years, a multitude of independent specialists, and many boxes of medical documentation.

I didn't care about the percentages or protocols. If there was some infinitesimal chance that I could receive a miracle, I was taking it. I was facing a life of paralysis. Who in my shoes wouldn't take that chance?

In the end, the miracle I received had nothing to do with statistics, rules, or debates about efficacy. It was about perspective. That's why, in a significant way, this chapter isn't just for the religious.

Sure, if you're a person of faith, you'll likely relate to this more than someone who is secular. Ultimately, however, I think everyone will understand the story I'm about to share.

This trip crystallized for me a notion I call "Compared to what?" It's a form of practicing perspective.

I learned a lot of that during my time at Craig Hospital, watching people with more severe injuries, such as brain trauma and complete paralysis. For what little function I may have had, I still had more than they did.

As much as I knew my situation could be worse, I also desperately wanted my body to be fully recovered. When you get an invitation to a place like Lourdes from an organization such as the Order of Malta, it can be intoxicating. The draw of hope is no small thing.

The fact that it coincided with the one-year anniversary of my injury only added to the allure, and May 6, 2018, fell on a Sunday. If the Lord was going to show Himself in the form of a miracle, this seemed like the perfect time.

Before going to Lourdes, I returned home to Sacramento and began the trip from there with my mom. The first leg was a quick flight to Los Angeles and then a direct flight from Los Angeles to Lourdes. That's about thirteen hours in the air.

Fueled by anticipation and desperation, I didn't sleep for a single moment on that flight. As the passengers around me dozed off, I was awake every minute, praying to God that I would receive a miracle, that I would somehow be healed. My longing to walk again was so intense that I cried many times, hoping God would hear me.

Lourdes is located in southwestern France, at the foot of the Pyrenees Mountains, near the border with Spain. To say it's beautiful is a vast understatement. The Catholic Church has made the area a shrine to the discovery by Saint Bernadette in 1858. When she was fourteen years old, she saw a vision of Mary in the grotto where the waters from the mountains emptied.

Bernadette saw the vision eighteen times, and Mary instructed her to drink from and bathe in the flowing water that appeared in the grotto. It is now the site of numerous miraculous healings, and the area has been a gathering point ever since, as the numbers indicate.

The pilgrimage to Lourdes is so popular that the church has implemented an organized entry system. Essentially, it's by appointment, although a couple hundred people line up at a time to await a chance to bathe.

The sick and injured people invited by the Order of Malta are called *malades*, which is simply the French term for a sick or injured person. As we malades waited in line, numerous volunteers from the church who spoke many different languages were there to help us.

The grotto area has several rooms in which people can bathe in the waters. After you get down to the water level, the volunteers help you undress. The process is very respectful to protect the privacy and dignity of the malades.

After I undressed, they laid me on my back, gave me a small figure of Mary to hold as I prayed, and lowered me into the water, which was fresh runoff from the snow on the mountains. It was freezing.

As I was lowered, I prayed as fervently as I could and begged, "Please, please, please, give me this miracle. Please, heal me." In that final moment of desperation, the freezing water caused my body to spasm and stiffen. My legs shot out uncontrollably and trembled as my body convulsed from a spasm. The volunteers brushed the water over me as they joined me in prayer.

But there was no healing.

There was no miracle where I got up, walked those steps, and danced around town. Nothing changed.

But that's only if you look at my body. My soul was a different matter. The miracle was really about spiritual and emotional healing. I gained strength by meeting other malades, many of whom were in more dire circumstances than mine. As I waited in line and met others, I heard one heartbreaking story after another.

Some of them had stage 4 cancer. One man told me: "I have tumors throughout my entire body. My doctors say I have just months to live. I have a beautiful wife and beautiful children who I love so much. I would give anything to have more time with them."

There was one malade there from Malibu, California. He had amyotrophic lateral sclerosis, which is better known as ALS or Lou Gehrig's disease. His body was slowly atrophying every day. He was still walking, albeit somewhat strenuously, using a cane to assist with his limp. But with ALS, it's only a matter of time before you're in a wheelchair, your body essentially completely crippled, but your mind still alert.

Most ALS patients die within a couple of years, and this man was in the countdown stage as the disease worked its way through his body. His speech was also impaired. He had to work for every word because of the paralysis in his tongue and mouth.

Like many others, he had a beautiful wife, beautiful kids, and every single day he was deteriorating. He said, "Robert, I won't be able to breathe on my own at some point, but I'll remain fully aware of what's going on."

When I hear things like that or remember my experience in Lourdes, I receive the miracle. I remind myself how lucky I am. How could I possibly dwell on my situation when these other human beings, these real people I'm connecting with, are telling me they would give anything to have what I have?

I'm not going anywhere. I had my trials in the beginning, and I struggled for my life. But now, I don't wake up uncertain about whether I'll live another day. That's guaranteed to the same extent as many of us.

I just want to walk again and regain my full independence. Many of the people I met at Lourdes weren't concerned with independence. They just wanted to live another day and be with their families. They wouldn't be upset to say, "I *have* to work out." They'd be excited they *get* to work out. They wouldn't be upset if they *had* to get out of bed early. They'd be excited that they're just able to get out of bed. They'd give anything to wake up each day and revel in the gift of life I still possess.

As I was in Lourdes, reflecting on these conversations, I spoke with a priest about my newfound perspective as we sipped a couple of beers. He was Father John Love, from

Santa Barbara, California. I explained this to Father Love and described the mental tools that had helped me with my challenges. We were having a really candid conversation.

It was something taking root in my soul, seeing all these people on this trip dealing with different ailments. The empathy and heartbreak I felt for them were deeply moving. It was in that conversation that we came up with this phrase, "Compared to what?"

Sure, I could say, "I'm so tired," but compared to what? "This is a really difficult situation that I deal with," but compared to what? Compared to what so many others face, there is so much that I can do in my life.

This statement and this perspective are not meant to dismiss my challenges or the challenges that someone else faces. That would be unhealthy. If we dismiss or ignore our challenges, they will never go away.

This phrase is meant to put our adversities into perspective, helping us realize that what we deal with can be overcome. We can overcome complex challenges and achieve immense goals, especially when we understand there are millions of people who would rather be in our situation than their own. "Compared to what?" is empowering.

Beyond that conversation and overall experience, there was one more moment in Lourdes that revolutionized my perspective.

On the one-year anniversary of my injury, I ascended a hill to pray at the fourteen Stations of the Cross with a small group. It's a path around a hill in Lourdes that guides you through the events of Jesus's Passion and crucifixion. You begin with Jesus standing before Pontius Pilate, condemned to death, while the crowd chants for Barabbas's release. You then move through the events of Jesus carrying the cross to His crucifixion.

The stations stood on a steep hill with a gravel path. Not exactly ideal conditions for a wheelchair, as you can imagine. I assumed it would be impossible for me to join the group, but a few people offered help when we discussed it over breakfast that morning. There were two volunteers from the Order of Malta, Scott Lukens and Ryan Tiernan, along with the bishop of the Sacramento archdiocese, Jaime Soto, and a malade named Edgar Gonzalez, along with his wife, Gioia.

Edgar had cancer. He had just completed his final round of chemotherapy and had only one functioning lung. Climbing a single flight of stairs left him breathless. He had no visible hair—no eyebrows, no eyelashes, and not a single strand on his head. Nothing. He joked about how he normally had a bushy unibrow. He was always upbeat and made everyone laugh, but you could tell he was fighting for his life.

Yet there he was, pushing me up a steep gravel road. Bishop Soto, who was sixty-two at the time, was also helping as we navigated the hills. I mean, these people were tired. Each time we stopped at one of these gorgeous, life-sized stations, I could hear them huffing and puffing, but they were determined for me to experience it. We continued on, and near the end, we reached a small cave that led into the mountain.

It didn't look wheelchair accessible. I thought I had already worked these guys hard enough, so I just let my mom and Edgar's wife go see it. My mom came back with tears running down her face. She said, "You need to see this." We found another way to get through the tunnel, though it was only marginally easier. This would still be quite a challenge for the guys helping me.

They rubbed their hands together and somehow pushed

me into this natural structure. Inside, water ran along the ceiling, slowly dripping down. I saw a statue of Mary holding Jesus in her arms. Jesus lay lifeless; Mary had one arm raised, gazing up at the sky, weeping.

As we looked at the statue, my mom broke down in tears and held me. I could barely hold back the tears welling in my eyes. The sorrow on Mary's face was so emblematic of what my mom was going through.

Through all the incredible support I have received, my mom has been there for me more than anyone. She slept in a chair by my bedside every night for two months, and when hospital staff told her she needed to leave the room, she slept in the lobby, praying I would survive the night. She was someone I could talk to, she scratched my nose when it itched, and she wiped my tears when I cried.

In Colorado, she spent eight months dedicating every moment to helping me. We celebrated together on my best days, and we cried when my defenses were beaten down. She spent her entire adult life giving my brother and me the best lives possible, and I can only imagine the pain she felt watching me struggle. She is, and always will be, a person I know will be there for me.

She is the ultimate example of unconditional love in my life. Witnessing this representation at the beautiful shrine in Lourdes, depicting Mary's love for Jesus, showed me just how much my mother loves me and, by extension, how much Mary loves me.

I sensed the love not only of my mom, but of these people—one of whom had only one functioning lung—who were helping me on this trip. They all had their own problems, and they had no history of personal connection to me. They could have easily said, "Yeah, this place just isn't accessible, and we unfortunately can't give you this experience.

Sorry." They didn't say that. Their love showed me the magnitude of the love Jesus has for me and all of us.

As our trip to Lourdes neared its end, all the malades gathered for a discussion. It was my turn to speak. I shared with them my experience of going through the Stations of the Cross and how Edgar helped me. I came to a realization that I was finally able to say out loud.

It was the first time I admitted that I might not walk again and truly meant it.

It was May 6, 2018, exactly one year after my injury. Before that, I had never admitted that I might not walk again and had actually come to terms with it. I had said it a few times to get therapists off my back. During rehab, when I talked about walking again, most therapists cautioned me. "Hope for the best, but prepare for the worst," they'd say. The sentiment came from a good place, but I didn't want to hear it. I didn't want any doubt in my mindset.

As I sat before my fellow malades, I finally came to grips with the fact that I might not walk again. I started crying and said, "I'll be OK with that because I know that no matter what happens to me, walking or not, I'm going to live a damn good life, and I'm going to be a damn good man."

Whether I'm moving from point A to point B on my feet doesn't matter because I know I have amazing people and God with me to carry me on this journey.

That experience was my healing. I didn't need to walk to live a good life. I didn't need to move my hands, dress myself, or feed myself to live a good life. I had all I needed through these living angels there to carry me through any challenge.

That was my miracle in Lourdes.

REFLECTION QUESTIONS

1. What is something you've overcome in the
   past that at one point felt impossible? What
   strengths did you uncover that can help you
   now?

2. Who is someone you know or have heard of
   who has faced an even tougher situation and
   still kept moving forward?

3. What are the positive aspects of your situation that others might wish they had?

Chapter 9

TAKE A STAND

Always take a stand for yourself, your values. You're
defined by what you stand for.

—Oprah Winfrey

T HIS PART HURTS to recount.
As I explained when discussing my mental diet, I
have been very intentional about not allowing negative thoughts into my headspace. I try to be cognizant
of when negativity enters my mind. When I recognize it,
I shut it down at the source. It's like an immune system
response to protect my mind.

What I struggled with most was the feeling of betrayal
by USA Rugby's leadership in the investigation of my
injury. Given months to consider an obvious problem that
should have become a teachable moment to protect the
game, they devised a baseless position that threatened the
players of the sport I love.

As this situation dragged on, I felt frustration bubble to
the surface of my consciousness. It became difficult to deal
with. People noticed my change in mood when I discussed
the issue. In those moments, the conversation shifted to a
serious note.

This was a negative subject, and I saw that as poison

to my mental diet. It distracted me from focusing on my goals. At the time, I was already fighting numerous battles just to survive. Thinking about how USA Rugby officials were twisting the narrative to serve their self-interest threatened my focus.

In the next chapter, I'll discuss forgiveness and how important it is to choose that path. I wholeheartedly stand by that. I forgive the leaders of USA Rugby for their actions, but that doesn't mean that what they did was excusable, quite the opposite, in fact. If everything had been handled the way it should've been, there would have been nothing to forgive in the first place.

I don't hold any anger in my heart, and in the end, USA Rugby issued a formal apology for its inadequate process and outcomes. I appreciate their apology and do not want it overlooked. That being said, I also don't want to gloss over the reality of the mistakes that were made and the emotional strain it had on me as it occurred. A transparent account of what happened and an explanation of its failures need to be made so it never repeats.

This is important because USA Rugby doesn't stand alone as the sole governing body with a history of mistakes. Look at USA Gymnastics and the National Women's Soccer League with sexual abuse scandals, the NFL with brain trauma cover-ups, and steroid use in the MLB. We see irresponsibility emerge again and again in the corporate world, whether it's the cigarette industry covering up the truth about lung cancer or Ford Motor Company ignoring safety concerns about its infamous Pinto in the 1970s.

There are countless examples of negligence, from individuals in government to corporations and academic institutions choosing the wrong path. For whatever reason, those in positions of authority don't always do the right thing, and it's up to members of the public to speak up and denounce those mistakes so they never happen again.

There comes a point when we have to stand by our values and what we care about. The injustice I experienced wasn't what hurt me the most. It was the missed opportunity to show the rugby community that the rules of the game exist for player safety, and when broken, an outcome like mine can occur.

Without that statement, it makes the actions that caused my injury seem admissible, and I couldn't bear the thought that every action wasn't taken to mitigate this from happening to someone else. If the leaders of USA Rugby wouldn't do that, the duty fell on my coaches, my family, and me to fill that void, even if that meant I had to revisit the feeling of betrayal.

In other words, the video and pictures of what happened to me should have been used as a lesson about how *not* to play and coach the game. It should have been used as reinforcement of rugby's laws against contact to the head and neck. It should have been part of a worldwide effort to make the game safer, to the extent that you can make a contact sport safe. This was a test of how the leaders of the game would handle a challenge that threatened the sport.

To be clear, my desire for an investigation was never about benefiting myself. I wasn't looking for personal gain. I didn't want money, nor did I have any desire to sue anyone.

A lawsuit wouldn't make me walk again. No matter how hard I work at my rehab, I will never play rugby again, so rule changes don't affect me personally. My legacy in rugby is about the safety of others.

That's a simple approach I thought the leaders of the

game would embrace. Instead, I watched adults in positions of authority, who had time and opportunity to do the right thing, fumble away the chance to make the best of a bad situation. When I look at it from an objective standpoint, this is a case study in failed leadership.

If you want to understand why USA Rugby went through a series of leaders over the past decade and ended up in bankruptcy proceedings by 2020, my story is a microcosm. That's not a jab. It's a real criticism of what happened with a group of people who didn't act responsibly.

This failure of justice was directed by select individuals in positions of authority, but those leaders who weren't directly involved and chose to remain silent are equally complicit. I always wanted to see USA Rugby do what was right. I love the sport and the American rugby community, which is why it hurt me so much to see the leaders who were supposed to support me turn their backs.

In the first few days after my injury, we focused on my health and survival. However, in the days after, it became clear that I had been seriously wronged.

Coach Clark and Coach Billups visited me multiple times in the hospital, starting the day of my injury and the day after, to check on me and show their support. Roughly a week later, they returned with serious news to share with my family and me. They showed my parents photos and videos captured by photographers and bystanders of the play in which I was injured. The images clearly showed a player from Arkansas State wrapping his arm around my neck, putting me in a headlock, and driving my skull into the ground.

The play was blatantly illegal.

Even if you don't understand the rules of rugby, a headlock is clearly dangerous. And it's not like we as rugby players hadn't been reminded of that. This is the exact kind of play that rugby's top officials were trying to eliminate.

Since the early days of rugby, contact around the head and neck has always been illegal, but prior to the start of the 2017 season, World Rugby, the sport's global governing body, increased its emphasis on penalizing this type of play. They emphasized two levels of penalty for making contact with the head and neck. Contact with the head or neck with a low degree of danger would result in a yellow card and a ten-minute suspension. For a high degree of danger, a red card would be issued, resulting in immediate expulsion from the game and a review for possible suspension from future matches. In either case, the offending player's team was forced to play shorthanded.

World Rugby wasn't playing around.

The release dealt with what are called "high tackles." While the play I was involved in wasn't technically a tackle, the rule prohibited contact above the shoulder level in all phases of play, specifically to prevent the type of injury that happened to me. Whether you call it a headlock, a grapple, or some other term, it was dirty.

Coach Clark sent the pictures and videos of my injury to USA Rugby with the obvious expectation that they would conduct an immediate and expeditious inquiry. The images clearly showed I was put in a headlock and the top of my head was driven to the ground. Clark even contacted USA Rugby to request an inquiry, though it seemed this should have been automatic given the severity of my injury and the clear evidence of its illegality.

The point was to make players and coaches more cognizant of the potential outcomes of their actions. I didn't break my neck tripping and falling.

But there was no immediate investigation. Clark

hounded the organization with requests for an inquiry. On June 7, 2017, roughly one month after my injury, USA Rugby informed him that an ad hoc committee had been formed to describe the sequence of events leading up to my injury.

The committee was led by Ed Todd, a USA Rugby staffer for appeals and grievances. Todd explained that the group's role was to gather facts and report its findings to the CEO of USA Rugby. He made it clear that this was in no way a disciplinary committee, so they had no power to impose or suggest sanctions as a result of their findings.

The committee consisted of a longtime Northern California rugby referee, John Coppinger; a Canadian-based anti-doping staffer, Tim Ricketts; an international athlete, Kitt Wagner Ruiz; and a USA Rugby referee manager, Richard Every.

Given the clear infraction that caused my injury, we assumed it wouldn't take long for this group to display the facts and then pass along the report to determine that a penalty had occurred and a red card violation should have been called. From there, every action would take place to condemn this sort of play and prevent it from occurring again. But again, our assumptions were wrong.

Days turned into weeks and weeks turned into months. I moved from Santa Clara Hospital to Craig Hospital. Purely by chance, USA Rugby's headquarters were just a few miles from Craig Hospital. That allowed the CEO of USA Rugby, Dan Payne, to visit me on a couple of occasions.

Payne initially struck me as a genuinely nice person. He seemed earnest and concerned about what had happened and about my recovery. I felt a sincere warmth from him.

In talking to him, I said that I didn't blame the sport of rugby for my injury, which I still don't.

Payne was later tempted to take that statement out of context and use it as an exoneration. He eventually sent a draft to Clark and told him that he wanted to release my statement on the USA Rugby website. Clark put his foot down.

"Here was Robert being Robert, a classy young man who didn't want to get into blaming anyone or wallow in anger, and Dan Payne wanted to take advantage of that," Clark says.

That's when I realized that I was in the middle of the politics of rugby. Payne had taken over in 2016 as USA Rugby was in the throes of its latest effort to grow. USA Rugby's leaders were working to portray rugby as a "safe" alternative to football, capitalizing on football's ongoing public relations issues. The NFL was still dealing with a massive class-action lawsuit over concussions and brain trauma.

USA Rugby saw this as an opportunity, arguing that the absence of helmets makes players less likely to put their head and neck in harm's way, thereby reducing the risk of head injuries. While there is some truth to that, let's not pretend. I played football and was recruited to play in college. I know the difference between injuries in football and rugby, and they are subtly different, not distinct. Rugby is still a contact sport played at high speed. The ability to deal with injuries and pain is part of the game. Serious injuries can and do happen in rugby. I'm proof of that.

If people are going to play the game, they need to understand that. If people are going to coach the game, they need to be vigilant in training athletes the right way. Don't pretend the sport is something that it's not.

The image of me getting paralyzed clashed head-on with how the game was being marketed. How are you supposed to tell parents that rugby is safer than football one day and then own up to a player getting paralyzed in an NBC nationally televised championship game?

Time dragged on, and Clark incessantly probed the status of the investigation. He wanted to know specifics, such as what materials would be reviewed, what the timeline was, and when interviews would be taking place. Clark wanted real answers, and Clark is not just a run-of-the-mill coach. He's the most successful US rugby coach in the sport's history. If he's reaching out, it is not a small issue.

Yet, Clark was getting excuses about what was going on, or he was getting stonewalled.

This should have been a simple investigation. But more days turned into more weeks and more months. My mom and I asked Payne to meet with us so we could get a sense of why this was taking so long. By this time, the initial warmth we shared became a distressed response from my mom and me. We no longer believed what he was saying.

Payne was lingering around what USA Rugby was going to eventually say after the inquiry. We were shocked. What could they say other than this was an overt violation of the rules and needed to be vigilantly dealt with? Then it started to dawn on us that USA Rugby might not say that at all.

During our last meeting, my mom and I looked at Payne with concern and said, "You can't possibly tell us that USA Rugby is going to issue a statement calling my injury a coincidence? You can't possibly say that there shouldn't have been a red card?"

And let me reiterate, I wasn't looking for a pound of flesh.

I didn't wish for the player who hurt me to be banned. I wasn't asking for Arkansas State or its coaches to be suspended. I was focused on progress for the sport and its current and future players, not punishment. Focusing on punishment was just going to take me down a dark path and that's the last thing I wanted.

Payne then said things like, "Well, I'm not in charge of the inquiry. It's an independent committee." I remember he said over and over, "I just want to do what's best for rugby." Finally, he said that he would issue a statement decrying what happened to me, regardless of the committee's results.

I was glad to hear that his focus was on what was best for rugby, but taking every action to prevent this injury from happening to someone else is clearly what's best for rugby, not dismissing it as an accident. His uncertainty about whether this sort of perilous play would be condemned by the organization was perplexing and disturbing.

My family and I were getting more and more frustrated. So was Clark. A process that should have taken a few days was becoming a never-ending bad dream. It was getting increasingly difficult for me to live with the stress this investigation put on my life.

On top of the politics surrounding the image and branding of rugby, the other problem was the criticism that was leveled at the team of three officials who refereed the match. People were wondering why the officials didn't pause the game after my injury occurred. Multiple phases of play unfolded while I lay motionless on the turf, screaming, with the game continuing just meters away from me.

Had someone landed on me in those first few moments,

my injury could have been more severe, possibly fatal. The only reason the game even paused was that we scored.

This incident should have been used as a teaching moment: When a player is motionless on the ground, play must stop immediately, regardless of their location on the field. But we don't know the reason for the referee team's inaction, and unfortunately, we never will because USA Rugby did not investigate this breakdown in officiating. Even though we were close to witnessing a death on the field, USA Rugby was so focused on sweeping this incident under the rug that they missed the opportunity to make the game safer.

The criticism of this officiating failure put the people who officiate rugby on the defensive. One of the members of the ad hoc committee was also a referee. The belief from Clark and others is that he essentially took control of the inquiry.

That's how USA Rugby ended up with a whitewashed report of what caused my injury. The results of the ad hoc committee were announced on August 7, 2017. The committee was instructed not to make disciplinary judgments, and in doing so, they used legal protection language to avoid the illegalities in the play. They even tried to place the blame on me.

When referring to the headlock around my neck, they stated the opposing player's "bind may be infringements of the laws." I was shocked to read that. How could wrenching someone to the ground by the neck not be a clear and dangerous violation?

When the opposing player made contact with me from the side of the maul, they explained that he moved his left arm into a "bind" over my neck and that he was "in a strong position to defend and drive into the maul." Strong position? Should "bind over the neck" and "strong position" be in the same report, much less the same sentence? I was dumbfounded to see a flagrantly illegal move described as strong.

They also detailed multiple times that I was guilty of having my shoulders below my hips, which is an infraction in rugby. They used this sort of language to suggest that my injury was due to my personal failure to keep my head up. They failed to explain that the sole reason for my body position was that my head was being driven downward because of the arm lock around my neck.

It was a slap in the face to my family and me. I felt betrayed by the leaders of the sport I love so much. How could they possibly make the premeditated decision to place the blame on me, the quadriplegic?

While we were appalled, USA Rugby seemed satisfied to stop the process there and issue a statement that their referee courses needed to be reviewed to reinforce the safety concerns in plays that have contact with the head or neck. Our focus was on doing everything possible to mitigate this injury from happening to anyone else, and their plan fell woefully short.

Clark pushed for a disciplinary committee to review the materials and determine whether a red card should have been issued. We hoped that a citing committee would avoid the safeguarding phrasing of the ad hoc committee's report and definitively condemn this kind of play. USA Rugby exhausted all options in trying to pass the task of citing to another organization.

They tried to push the referral to the championship tournament we competed in, then our conference, and then our division, each of which was either unable or unwilling to perform a citation review. Gary Heavner, a judicial officer appointed by USA Rugby to oversee collegiate rugby in our division, stated in writing that our match was a "wholly unsanctioned competition." As a result, he recused himself from the citing process.

This was nonsense. USA Rugby had given the Varsity Cup National Championship its full official sanction before the event occurred. Further, both Cal and Arkansas State were dues-paying members of USA Rugby in good standing, and our match was officiated by a USA Rugby-appointed referee.

The Varsity Cup tournament featured some of the most prestigious rugby programs and universities in America, including the military academies, BYU, Penn State, UCLA, Notre Dame, and other top-ranked schools. This was no breakaway, unsanctioned competition. Heavner's recusal was flawed and politically motivated.

Clark cautioned USA Rugby against each of these moves, but they proceeded anyway, wasting more time in the process. Eventually, they forwarded the referral to David Pelton, a volunteer USA Rugby referee who worked for a tech company and had become a "citing commissioner" for World Rugby.

On September 22, roughly four and a half months after my injury, Pelton's report was released with his final determination: No red-card penalty occurred. My family and I read the report in disbelief. If driving someone into the turf by their head and rendering them a quadriplegic isn't a red card, then what is?

Pelton admitted in his report that he did not contact me, Clark, the match officials, medical personnel, or the player and coach from Arkansas State. As he said in the report, he relied simply on what he saw from the pictures and video. He essentially rubber-stamped the ad hoc committee's report.

This is the critical passage from Pelton's report:

> Photographic evidence shows prior to the collapse there is less visible evidence of muscle strain (an indication of active attempt to pull down on the neck) than when both players are moving down as the maul collapses (see attachments 5 and 6). Based on the ability of Cal #5 to maintain a body position that had the neck in line with the shoulders (see attachment 5) there does not appear to be large force applied to the contact with the neck. In addition, given the constant position of the elbow in relation to the head there appears to be no torquing motion applied to the neck.

Clark, my parents, and I were furious. I have no idea what photos Pelton was looking at, but there are clear images where you can see the muscles flexing on the opposing player's arm as he held me in a headlock. You can also see the muscles in my neck flexing as I struggle to fight my head upward. How do you think a six-foot-five, 240-pound man is going to the ground without torquing?

On top of that, Pelton stated three separate times in the report that the reason he didn't interview anyone was because "Referral came four months after the match." That was a nonsense excuse.

Clark did everything in his power to move the process along swiftly, starting immediately after he got the photos and videos. Any delays were because of USA Rugby's lack of diligence and care.

But here's the other point about the timing of the referral: It doesn't matter. We could have waited a year to make the referral. If you're charged with doing an inquiry, you still make phone calls. You still perform a full assessment.

Decades-old cold cases get solved. You see them on TV all the time. To say that four months having passed was too long to gather testimonies was preposterous.

The bottom line is that it certainly appears Pelton and USA Rugby's leaders wanted a conclusion they felt would protect the organization. They did not at all appear concerned about me, the game itself, or, more importantly, the safety of every rugby player in America.

Or as Clark rhetorically asked years later, "Why would Pelton's views of the incident be of value, but the actual recollection of the match officials, perpetrator, victim, medical personnel, broadcast/media personnel, other players, coaches...not be relevant?" Clark continued, "Instead, what he did was use only his own opinion...[and] they even sanitized that Robert was in a headlock or arm lock around his neck by referring to it as a bind."

When you put together Pelton's groundless interpretation with his failure to do the smallest amount of diligence by calling the parties involved, you have a complete embarrassment for USA Rugby.

Until this moment, my family and I had never made a public statement about our disappointment with USA Rugby's leadership. I didn't want to expose myself to the trauma of the situation, and we wanted to give them every chance to do the right thing.

Once the results were revealed, we finally had to speak up. In most cases, I encourage others to find ways to prevent negative thoughts from entering their minds. Too much negativity can paralyze one's mindset.

However, there comes a time when an injustice becomes too great to ignore. The pain of knowing USA Rugby wasn't doing everything it could to prevent another injury like mine was greater than the pain of fighting against this. I either had to live with their failure for the rest of my life or speak up until this investigation was condemned. So, I crafted a message with my parents, and they immediately went on Facebook to criticize the inquiry.

"Without this incident deemed as illegal contact, it constitutes this action as excusable," we wrote. "We question what can or will be done to prevent this from happening again."

The post included photos and videos of the moment I was hurt, forcing me to relive it. Again, it was necessary for me to endure to show how wrong the investigation was. Through it all, Clark stood by my side and called out the organization in forthright terms.

"The USA Rugby decision is shameful and without merit," Clark wrote in an email to the *East Bay Times*. "The evidence clearly shows a lengthy flagrant penalty. Dangerous play such as this will result in serious injury more times than not. USA Rugby has failed Robert and failed the game."

To cap it all off, Payne never denounced the investigation after the determination came out. Everything he said to my mom and me was just to pacify us. Instead of doing what was best for the sport, he did what he thought was best for himself.

The botched inquiry became a flashpoint for those concerned about the leadership failures within USA Rugby. By 2018, there were more and more questions about the direction of the organization.

It was later revealed in bankruptcy filings that USA Rugby lost $4.4 million in 2017 and another $4.2 million in 2018. By April 2018, Payne resigned amid the growing problems and took over as CEO of Rugby Americas. In 2021, he was named the USA Rugby general manager of high performance.

As time went on, Clark never stopped demanding that this decision be appealed and the inadequate process be condemned. He sent more than one hundred emails over the entirety of the process, relentlessly browbeating the CEO, chairman, vice chairman, and board of directors of USA Rugby. As leaders left the organization and new ones took their places, Clark would call on them to denounce the investigation and its outcomes, but his requests were met with silence or excuses.

Frustrated by the lack of response, Clark took to social media to voice his discontent. He posted detailed accounts of the investigation's shortcomings, calling for transparency and justice. His posts immediately gained community support. Players, coaches, and fans shared his posts, wrote letters of their own to the board, and expressed their solidarity.

We continued to demand that USA Rugby review the inquiry process and do what was right. It took years and multiple changes in leadership, but it eventually happened. On June 15, 2020, USA Rugby issued the following statement:

> Over the past three years, USA Rugby's Board of Directors and National Office have fielded inquiries regarding Robert Paylor's injury (University of California), issues surrounding a lack of action and an inadequate process around the post-injury investigation and citing. The current USA Rugby Board, alongside several members of the National Office has reviewed USA Rugby's handling of the catastrophic injury.

First, on behalf of USA Rugby, we apologize to Robert Paylor and his family for the lack of timely action and an inadequate citing process. We agree that retrospectively, the citing process should have been more transparent, provided more rigorous due diligence and openly communicated to all parties involved.

As a result of the outcome, USA Rugby determined that all catastrophic injuries will require an immediate, independent panel review for foul play, including but not limited to mandatory interviews and review of video evidence. We must be intensely focused on upholding the laws of the game and player welfare is paramount to our success as a sport.

The Varsity Cup was a USA Rugby sanctioned event that was organized by a third party. The universities and players, including Robert Paylor, were members of the union in good standing. Robert deserved our organization's best efforts and the process didn't meet anyone's expectations.

Again, on behalf of USA Rugby, we apologize to Robert Paylor and the entire Paylor Family for how the case was handled, as a whole. We are sorry that an incident of this magnitude did not receive the expedient action and transparency it deserved. It resulted in outcomes that were subpar and left Robert and his family confused and frustrated. USA Rugby's current Board of Directors is taking the proper steps to ensure that corrective actions are in place to prevent any reoccurrence.

I haven't received a personal apology from any members of the ad hoc committee, Payne, or Pelton, but we were satisfied that USA Rugby deemed their work inadequate. It took years of grappling with the negativity the case cultivated, but I'm relieved that current and future rugby players will play on safer terms due to learning from my injury.

If I do nothing else in this chapter, I want people to understand that I love rugby and the people who play it. I will do anything I can to promote and protect the sport. I'm not bitter about getting hurt. I even encouraged my brother to keep playing after what happened to me.

USA Rugby's mistakes should serve as a learning opportunity for leaders about what not to do. When there's a problem, deal with it. Don't shy away from it. It's like the old saying: "The cover-up is always worse than the crime."

When USA Rugby made that mistake after my injury, it was disheartening. But in the end, the persistence to stand up to injustice prevailed and freed me from the anguish tied to the inquiry. It's not easy, but a chronic negative influence in your life can't be ignored. It needs to be addressed and neutralized, or that problem will linger forever.

It took four years of grappling with a situation that brought me grief, but finally, the blame game is over.

REFLECTION QUESTIONS

1. Have there been times in your life when you regret not standing up for something or someone? What would you do differently now?

2. How can you improve transparency and accountability in your own actions and leadership? Are there ways you find yourself deviating from your values?

Chapter 10

CHOOSE FORGIVENESS

*Anger is an acid that can do more harm to the vessel in which
it is stored than to anything on which it is poured.*

—MARK TWAIN

THE JOURNEY FROM rage to forgiveness is difficult.
Of all the battles I've faced, overcoming the
intense anger I felt toward the person who hurt me
may have been the most difficult. The emotions of my new
reality and physical limitations were obviously difficult to
face, but there was usually no choice. The battle against
pneumonia was physically brutal, but it was ultimately a
decision between life and death. There was no choice to be
made in my mind.

Rehabilitation has been constant and both physically
and emotionally exhausting. But it's also the difference
between having purpose or not. Again, that's not a choice
for me. I need purpose.

But there was something very different about the process of overcoming rage. The confluence of my anger at
feeling abused and ignored collided with my spiritual
upbringing and my intellect in a unique way. I had a
choice to go one way or another.

I could let my rage play out and dictate the rest of my

life. It was an easy trap to fall into and would, quite honestly, allow that state of mind to control me. That rage had power because of what had been done to me.

In the end, however, the journey to forgiveness proved to be critically important. It has kept me focused on my greater purpose because the most important lesson about forgiveness is that it's a two-way transaction. You truly get back what you give.

In offering forgiveness for how I was wronged, I received a profound sense of peace. Let me tell you though, the rage was real, and it was as tempting as it was destructive.

The other point I want to make is that some people may come away from reading this chapter feeling like I still have that rage. I don't, but it's easy to sense that because of how I recount what happened to me and how I had to process it. Truthfully, while I publicly forgave the person who hurt me right away, releasing those negative attachments internally took a lot longer.

The more I was told about the person who hurt me and about how or why he reacted the way he did, the more twists and turns there were to the process of complete forgiveness. I say that because you may experience the same hurdles as you work through your own process of forgiveness.

I want to be as realistic as possible about the journey. I'm not trying to embarrass or cause this person to feel guilty after all these years. This is not some passive-aggressive attempt at revenge. Specifically, I will never mention this person's name, and I insist that people don't go searching for him. That's the complete opposite of my goal for this chapter. This is not about trying to draw that person out for public ridicule or punishment. At the same time, I don't want to gloss over the events that unfolded or the emotions I felt in dealing with them.

This chapter is to help people who feel that they have been wronged. Almost everyone can relate to that feeling. While I don't believe there was an intention to break my neck, my injury was not caused by a fluke either. I didn't break my neck using poor form or mistiming a tackle. I didn't just lose my balance.

There was a combination of key decisions made that caused my injury. It could and should have been avoided. Knowing that it wasn't was hard to deal with. Yet, there was nothing I could do to change that and I needed to process my emotions, particularly after what I found out days later.

As I was lying in the hospital for the first few days, I couldn't recall the exact series of events that led to my injury. For anyone who's played high-level contact sports, not remembering exactly what happened in detail isn't surprising. I was injured in a collision of bodies that comprised a maul. It's a giant mass of human collision, and when I say that mauls are dark and chaotic, I mean that literally. There were roughly fifteen players engaged in this maul, which created a physical blur of contact points, and the whole play unfolded in only a matter of seconds.

However, it appeared that intentionally collapsing this maul could have been part of their coaching strategy. Our team was highly effective in the maul that year and had a strong reputation for forming mauls with a high success rate. A game plan to bring us down by any means necessary to stop us from scoring, even if it meant taking a penalty, didn't seem like an implausible strategy on their part, despite how dangerous it is.

Additionally, the player from Arkansas State was a lot

smaller than me. I was half a foot taller and probably out-weighed him by forty to fifty pounds. I'm sure he was doing whatever he could to bring us down. In this case, he broke a serious rule.

But when I say that I didn't really know how I had gotten hurt, other than my head was driven into the turf, that's the truth. Even when I watched the replay on NBC Sports, I couldn't really tell. The overhead angle from the press box camera didn't show much.

After Coach Clark and Coach Billups brought the new pictures and videos of my injury to my family and me, the puzzle came together.

I had empirical evidence that the cause of my injury was flat-out illegal. This was one of the most important rules in the game, and for obvious good reason. Just mere contact with the head or neck is a clear line in the sand. Let alone driving a player's head into the turf. Anyone who has played or follows rugby knows that.

Unrelenting physical domination and intimidation define rugby's battle of wills, proving who is more com-mitted and unbreakable. The most tenacious men and women play our sport, but when you step onto the rugby pitch, there's an unwritten contract that at no point in time will you do anything to maim an opponent. The head, eyes, and spine are all off-limits for even the hardest athletes on the planet.

I had witnessed my fair share of rugby injuries before, but nothing like this. The worst I had seen were dislocated shoulders, torn ACLs, or broken bones. You feel horrible when you see something like that, but know that these aren't usually permanent, life-changing injuries. As prev-alent as collisions are in rugby, spinal cord injuries are virtually unheard of. Also, I had never seen an opponent make an illegal move that directly caused a serious injury. That added an undeniable layer of indignation.

I've talked about how rare an injury like mine is with Coach Clark before, and when you do the math, it becomes clear my injury wasn't an accident.

Clark has coached approximately a thousand games over his more than forty years of coaching, and each match probably consists of roughly ten mauls. Out of these ten thousand total mauls, roughly 70 percent of them collapse, so he's witnessed about 7,000 collapsed mauls, yet only one instance of a broken neck resulting from it—mine. What set my case apart from the 6,999 others was that they didn't have someone wrenching a player down by their neck. If they had, there would have been a lot more paralyzed rugby players.

I knew that between the player from Arkansas State and the team of three match officials, this wasn't supposed to happen. The officials didn't stop play and, worse, the player did it. When you combine how I was supposed to be protected with the emotional trauma of being paralyzed, you had a recipe for rage.

And I certainly felt it.

Pure, unadulterated rage. It enveloped me, sending me into a spinning mess just as I was trying to cope with the initial shock of my new reality and the physical exhaustion of battling pneumonia.

My mind drowned in the thoughts of all that I was suffering. I couldn't breathe or swallow, numbness tingled throughout my body, and I wrestled with the constant fear that my independence could potentially be stripped away forever. I should have been standing with my teammates at the end of that game, raising the trophy, and wearing the medals we had just won as national champions. I should have gone back to Cal that night to celebrate.

I should have been walking on clouds of victory instead of lying in a state of infirmity.

I wasn't supposed to face a life of paralysis. I was supposed to be on my life's journey to success and happiness the way I had planned it. This injury wasn't my fault. This wasn't an unfortunate anomaly. There was definitive proof that all my pain and suffering were because of the actions of another person.

This was the first step in the process, and it was ugly for me. My dad felt the pain as well. Making it worse for me was that I couldn't take that anger out in a healthy way. I couldn't go for a run or lift weights to release the rage. There was just me, lying in that bed with nothing but time to think.

The initial answer for me in dealing with this rage was about faith. I was raised Catholic and am still a practicing Catholic. I was taught to forgive people for their mistakes regardless of how horrible the wrongdoing or how angry I felt.

This created a moral dilemma within me. My initial instinct was to cling to the rage. I saw plenty of reasons to justify that decision, and I think most people probably would have agreed with me. There are lots of people who use rage to fuel their motivation.

But deep down, I knew in my heart that I would be going against my faith and principles if I took that path. I felt that this was a test of whether I would stand by those principles or stray away when it was most difficult. If I couldn't forgive the player out of my own desire, I had to do it for God.

I remembered my spiritual director's advice before my

spinal fusion surgery, that I could control my mindset regardless of my circumstances. I couldn't turn off this rage like a light switch, but regardless of what I felt internally, I could always control my words and actions.

As hard as it was, I decided to begin the path of healing by saying I forgive this person in every conversation I had going forward. I wouldn't give words to my anger and let it control me.

My path to healing was clear, but it was anything but easy. Most people ask for forgiveness. The player from Arkansas State never did.

He never called me or said he was sorry. Neither has his coach. As I write this book eight years later, neither has contacted me. Some people from the Arkansas State rugby community reached out, but not the player, the head coach, or their director of rugby.

That was the next part of this journey. It was the feeling that this person was not only careless, but he also lacked compassion. That's a rough assessment of someone I didn't know and had never spoken to. But I didn't know what he was or wasn't thinking because my mind was left to imagine. I had no context other than my feeling of being wronged and silence from him.

That contributed to the ebb and flow of my journey to forgiveness. This wasn't a linear progression where I felt a little bit better about it each day. On days when I had a difficult treatment or workout, my rage would climb. Forgiveness didn't happen overnight, and there wasn't one moment I remember when I was suddenly at peace.

The journey to reaching that sense of peace lasted six months or so. The process was gradual, and not hearing from him only prolonged it, leaving me to wonder why he wouldn't reach out. Over the years, I heard a couple of explanations. Neither was satisfactory, which made things more challenging.

A couple of days after the game, Coach Clark reached out to Arkansas State's director of rugby to check on the other player. Essentially, Clark wanted to know if the other player was doing OK mentally and make sure he wasn't ravaged by guilt.

Clark told me the director's reaction was along the lines of, "What guilt should he feel?" The director said there were a number of factors that went into me getting hurt and that this one player wasn't responsible for the outcome.

To claim that an illegal headlock wasn't the decisive factor in my paralysis is willfully ignorant. If that same situation had played out without my head being forced to the ground, I would have fallen safely and none of this would have happened.

Ignoring that fact is not what's best for the sport and those who play. Moreover, the director purely lacked compassion for an opponent. We're not just pawns in a game that coaches play. We're people, and one of those people had his life completely turned upside down.

That explanation perplexed me, and a conversation a year later with one of the player's former coaches confirmed it. He is a big supporter of rugby in Texas. Moreover, he was very vocal on social media in criticizing USA Rugby over how the organization handled the investigation into my injury.

I ran into the former coach at the 2018 Rugby World Cup Sevens in San Francisco. He came up to me with so many words of encouragement and examples of how my journey had inspired him. Then, he mentioned that he had coached the player who injured me. I asked why the player hadn't called me, especially since I had been so public in forgiving him.

He essentially explained that the player had been convinced my injury was nothing more than a fluke. He was told a message similar to what Clark received from Arkansas State's director of rugby, that there were lots of factors in what led to my injury and his action wasn't the determining cause.

If I still had rage, this would have been more fuel for that fire. Instead, the good thing for me is that I was well down the path of forgiveness. Whenever people asked me if I forgave the person who hurt me, I continued to say yes. I never missed a beat.

Did I always feel like forgiving him? Certainly not always. Yet the more I spoke those words, the more it eased my rage. As time went on, I didn't have the same internal reaction as when I was in the hospital.

I was told the player felt deep remorse but was advised by legal counsel to stay silent, fearing it might be seen as an admission of guilt. I don't see that as a valid reason to never reach out. Calling to say you're sorry I got hurt is not an admission of guilt. We're also more than five years outside of the statute of limitations. When you don't reach out at all, that makes you look uncaring. Or it makes you appear more guilty, not less.

Let me be clear, I was never going to sue anybody. Pursuing legal action would have kept me focused on the past and getting revenge. I wanted to move on and direct my focus toward my rehabilitation.

I just wanted some closure. I wanted to heal. I wanted to continue my journey of forgiveness and move on. Fortunately, I was surrounded by people who did care and who did love me.

This is where I started to really grasp the notion of forgiveness. By repeatedly saying that I forgave this person, I stripped away the power from those feelings of anger. By not adding fuel to the fire of rage, it slowly burned out. As I worked through that process internally, it allowed me to consider the intellectual side of the equation.

By thinking instead of reacting, I could reflect, what good is this rage doing for me? That didn't stop the rage right away, but it made me think. Was the rage helping me heal? No. Was the rage getting me into the right state of mind to fight for my life and my future? No.

The rage was nothing but emotions. It wanted me to vent about something that wasn't going to change. This player from Arkansas State played the critical role in my injury, but I couldn't dwell on the past if I wanted to move forward. My body was paralyzed, and I needed to see what was in front of me, not be distracted by what was behind me.

The rage I felt back then was never going to get me anywhere. Sure, for some people rage can be a fire for motivation. But I think you run the risk of anger making that fire get out of control. When that happens, you get burned, and it can spread to other areas of your life. I can't imagine what my life and relationships would look like if I had harbored that hate over all these years.

I've chosen the path of internal peace, and I am so proud and grateful that I made that daily choice. My focus is on the future, how I can make a difference in people's lives, and carry out my life's work. I'm not stuck thinking about what I've lost; I'm able to see what I've retained and gained. This journey has shown me that the true gift of forgiveness is more about personal healing than washing away guilt from someone else. It's about removing negative attachments from the person who was wronged.

Staying on the path to removing those attachments requires the realization that forgiveness isn't just a feeling correlated with the peace that comes from moving on from a negative interaction. Forgiveness is also a decision. Because I chose to make that decision day after day, I am now free. It's this realization that liberates us.

The journey can be difficult, long, and it may have setbacks, but we can all reach that peace if we choose to give power to only three transformational words:

I forgive you.

Reflection questions

1. Is there someone in your life you need to forgive? Do you need to forgive yourself for something? Or is there a situation that you can't control that's holding you back?

2. What emotions are you holding on to, and how are they impacting your mindset and daily life?

3. In what ways can you start to speak and act with forgiveness, even if you don't fully feel it yet?

Chapter 11
ADAPT AND OVERCOME

*You must be willing to leave the life that you planned
in order to find the one waiting for you.*

—Joseph Campbell

I CAME BACK TO the clanging and the thudding.
 I spent more than a year rehabilitating and fighting
to get my life back. I was determined to return to college, return to the life I imagined, and chase my dreams.
I even had a vision that I would be walking by the time I
got back to school, marching through Cal's Sproul Plaza
and past historic Sather Gate into the middle of campus.

Although I wasn't walking, I was finally back in the
exact place I wanted to be. From my first day in the hospital, I dreamed of returning to Berkeley. What I also got
was a dose of reality that tested my focus and perspective. My return to Cal was both amazing and challenging.
I was ecstatic to get back to school, surrounded by my
friends, and back to having my life on track.

At the same time, I had to learn to find joy in the little
things because the challenges were all around me.

Little things like the sounds of weightlifting or the bellowing of a truck horn at the crack of dawn. Or keeping
perspective on the fact that while my life wasn't where I

had hoped, I was still at one of the greatest universities in the world. I had a chance to do something that millions of other people would beg for.

I wasn't going to let the new obstacles I faced get me down. At the same time, some obstacles can paralyze you mentally as much as physically. Lots of people look at my positive outlook and think these obstacles don't affect me. Trust me, I grapple with them too.

I get how daily annoyances can become burdensome, such as trying to carry too much at once and dropping it or reaching for a coffee mug just out of reach. There were, and sometimes still are, somber moments when my frustrations got the best of me.

For me, the issues of my disability were obvious, like the humiliation that went with not being able to control my bodily functions in the simplest ways. If I have to urinate, I have no control over stopping it. Other simple tasks like throwing on a T-shirt and shorts to go to class went from a two-minute routine to a forty-five-minute event. Combing my hair? I kept a buzz cut to simplify my life.

Still, I believe each of us holds the power to overcome whatever setbacks paralyze us from pursuing our goals, whether it's losing weight or striving for a promotion.

No matter how clear our vision or consistent our efforts, things rarely go as planned. The only certainty in life is uncertainty, and when life doesn't progress the way we hoped, we have to adapt and find a way to keep persevering.

Maybe you're pursuing a fitness goal and face an injury. Will you give up entirely, or will you adjust your training to focus on what you can still do? Will you pivot your attention to rehabilitation, or let this unexpected obstacle define you?

In business, market shifts can paralyze even the best

strategists. The COVID-19 outbreak in 2020 tested the resilience of countless businesspeople. Could they pivot quickly enough? Could they make critical decisions between investing in their business or cutting back on labor hours?

Maybe you want to write a book or a screenplay. How do you get past writer's block or overcome the criticism that comes with editing? Worse, how do you deal with the likely rejection you may face along the way from publishers?

Jack Canfield and Mark Victor Hansen faced relentless rejection in the early 1990s with a book they had written. Every New York publisher they met with rejected their idea. They ended up at a small publisher in Florida. Almost thirty years later, they turned the original idea for the book *Chicken Soup for the Soul* into more than 250 titles. They eventually grew their idea into a publicly traded company.

For me, coming back to college showed me just how significant my physical challenges had become. The sixteen months between my injury and returning to school were anything but easy. At the same time, I always had help, and I didn't spend a minute alone.

Whether it was my mom, dad, brother, or the many doctors, nurses, and therapists, someone was always by my side. They were there through the dire moments, such as my battle with pneumonia. They were there for the mundane problems, such as when I dropped my cell phone.

When I returned to Cal, I didn't want to hire a caregiver. I had worked hard at building my independence, so I wanted to use those regained abilities to get myself through each day. Did I know it would test me? Yes. But if I could get through that first year after my injury, I believed I could overcome whatever challenges came my way in the future.

Those challenges turned up the first day I was on my own. My parents and brother were joined by Coach Clark, Coach Billups, and my rugby teammates to move me into my new apartment in Berkeley. I was so happy to see them. Finally, I was back. I remember they put my room together for me, I thanked everybody and then told my teammates I'd see them later that night. They went back to their houses and that's when it hit me.

I just dove into the deep end of the pool. When you're paralyzed and you drop your cell phone under your desk or bed, it's a test of dexterity with a stick to get it back. Throw in the mobility problems I had with controlling the stick and it was sometimes enough to make me lose my cool. The first time I tried to put on my shoes, it took me an hour.

I needed help with tasks like doing my laundry or taking out the garbage. The things I took for granted in life became a hardship. Meals were also interesting because there was no asking my mom to help make me something.

My mom was great because she'd do a lot of meal prepping for me. She'd make a bunch of chicken dishes, lasagna, or other dinners and package them individually, freeze them, and bring them to me when she or my dad visited. I had a freezer in my room, so all I had to do was put some food in the microwave. Cooking from scratch was too much of a challenge and far too risky for getting a burn.

But I still had to transport the food from the kitchen to my room. I'd have the plate on my lap as I pushed my wheelchair to my room. If my legs spasmed, the food would end up on the floor.

If I went out to a restaurant, sometimes the bathrooms weren't accessible. I'd have to hustle back to my room, and this is where it would get really humiliating. For many people who are paralyzed, bladder control is a significant issue.

If I had to hustle back to my apartment, I ran the risk that I might not get back in time. I ended up wetting my pants almost every day. Diapers and incontinence pads helped to minimize the need to change clothes every time, but what college student wants to wear those?

I remember many times when something went wrong, and I'd be staring at food on the floor or at my urine-soaked clothes. I'd just say to myself, "What the hell happened to me?" Add these challenges on top of studying at one of the most academically demanding colleges in the world and you can find yourself nearing a spiral of depression over something you can't control.

There were moments when I felt discouraged. Because of my disability, I wasn't able to live with my friends. As is common in Berkeley, they all lived in places that had stairs. I ended up living with two guys I didn't know. They were great people, but they were transfer students who had their own focus on getting to know the Cal campus and getting through school.

We were roommates more out of convenience than connection. We didn't have the late-night banter that you have in college or the moments when you stay up playing video games together and shooting the breeze.

I saw my friends and teammates practically every day, but I had to eventually face my reality. Toward the end of the day, it was just me in my room, lying in bed late at night with my eyes open. Trying to sleep was often a losing battle as I worked to calm my racing mind. When I was in class, my workouts, or hanging out with friends, I was truly happy. I was exactly where I wanted to be with the people who made me feel great. At night, I didn't have those distractions.

Inevitably, my thoughts would drift to that moment when I got hurt. I had this three-second video clip on my phone of the exact moment when I broke my neck. There were nights that I would just play it over and over and over and over again, still bewildered by how much my life had changed because of that one moment. Sometimes I watched it for an hour at a time.

Other times, I watched a feature the Pac-12 Network had done on my recovery. It was an amazing piece, but there was this difficult moment for me when it showed me lying on the field, my parents rushing to me and my dad grabbing my hand. I know he had my hand in his, but I couldn't feel it. That was one of the first moments when I knew just how much trouble I was in and how it affected those who loved me. When I watched those moments, I wasn't really thinking. I was just feeling.

These were life-changing events that couldn't be ignored. They needed to be processed and grieved. This was an important part of coming to terms with my injury, but that state of grief was a place I knew I couldn't stay in. I needed to keep my life moving forward.

Fortunately for me, I had so many more positives to be grateful for and could keep myself busy. Not just active, but intellectually challenged by the fantastic rigors of being back and living an intentional life. My first year back, which was my junior year, I was taking four classes a semester. I was doing rehab every day and going to the Haas School of Business, which was a very new, exciting experience.

By my senior year, I was taking six classes a semester because I wanted to graduate in four academic years, and I was developing my inspirational speaking business. I was finding my new purpose and building a life that I truly loved, so the moments I drifted off were far more limited.

On a daily basis, people would come up to me as I went around campus. They wanted to wish me well or let me know how I'd inspired them. I'm an extroverted person, so I feed off interacting with people. The energy I got from others made up for the hardships, including the process of wheeling around campus.

Then there was one day that I was rolling down the street on the way to a rehabilitation session. This was one of the days when I'd get up at six o'clock and get after it, wheeling myself down the sidewalk. While I had teammates who would help me get around Berkeley, I didn't want to ask anybody to get up for those early workouts.

The challenging thing about my wheelchair is that it was self-propelled, for the most part. I didn't want a motorized wheelchair because I wanted to keep working on my upper body. I did have an attachable electric motor to help me around the Berkeley hills. Between the motor and my teammates, I got everywhere I needed to go.

Anyway, getting to my seven o'clock workout was on me. That morning, I was cruising down the sidewalk with my eyes half closed when this semitruck horn bellowed right next to me. It shocked me and I looked over. The truck driver was pumping his fist out of the window and cheering me on. I absolutely loved it. Those little moments can get you through a lot of hardship.

Again, if you don't control your mindset, it's easy to get overwhelmed by the constant reminders of how your life hasn't gone the way you planned. If you're trying to get stronger or lose weight, you're almost certainly going to hit a plateau. How do you deal with the temptation of putting in less effort when you're not noticing any progress?

If you're building a business, how do you deal with an unexpected recession or maybe a regulator that surprises you with an enforcement issue? Those challenges are every day. For me, it could be something as simple as seeing scooters.

Yes, scooters.

On a sprawling campus like Cal, having a motorcycle or scooter is practically a survival tool for a college athlete. You don't have a lot of time. You sometimes have to go a long distance from one end of campus to the practice field, then back to a workout at the gym, race for dinner, and hustle to get some studying in. On top of that, your body is beat, so you just want an easy way to get around.

Scooters are the answer. I knew that before I ever got to campus.

Before I headed to Cal as a freshman, my dad and I took lessons so I could get my license. We went to a motorcycle course in Sacramento. Mind you, this was in the summer when temperatures regularly hover over a hundred degrees in the valley. This was also a training facility where their rule was "No skin below the chin." That means no bare skin of any kind can be exposed below your chin.

My dad and I were cloaked in boots, jeans, long-sleeved shirts, gloves, and helmets. Not exactly a summer outfit. It felt like being sealed in a roasting bag and thrown in an oven. You get done with four hours of riding on what seems like molten-hot blacktop and you're ready for an ice bath.

Then there was the ridiculously funny part where I had to train on a 50cc scooter. By the time I got to Cal, I had a 150cc scooter because a 50cc scooter is not exactly going to move a person my size, especially not around the notoriously steep Berkeley hills.

But when I was training, I looked like Jim Carrey from *Dumb and Dumber* on that 50cc scooter. My legs were completely bowed out as I was trying to learn how to maneuver this tiny bike. The instructors were really into it as well. They told me to lean hard into the turns as if I were in a high-speed motorcycle race.

I was thinking to myself, "Guys, I'm just figuring out how to get to the library a little quicker. I'm not preparing for the Isle of Man motorcycle race." I felt like I was about to scrape my kneecap off at any time. One of the instructors joked that they should have made me clutch a football between my knees to keep my legs tucked. It was a great, funny memory of something I did with my dad.

By the time I got to Cal with my 150cc scooter, I was ready to star in a remake of *Easy Rider*. I cruised around campus and parked in the long line of scooters in front of the Simpson High Performance Center, the training facility for varsity athletes that we call the HPC.

It was one of those little things about college that made me feel like I belonged to a special group. After my injury, that was gone, replaced by a wheelchair. Every time I went to the HPC, I saw that line of parked scooters and felt a twinge about what I had lost.

I had to catch myself and think, "Are you going to let that twinge take control of you? Or are you going to block that out and be grateful that you're here?" If I let a little thing like that defeat me, where would I be today?

I focused on what I had, not what I lost. I thought of the patients I'd met at Craig Hospital, the malades in Lourdes, and countless others I'd encountered along the way. I

155

reminded myself that there were people who would beg for the opportunities I had in front of me.

Was I really going to let the memory of riding a scooter spiral to the end of my battle for a better life? "Come on," I told myself, "lift your head up." Instead of thinking about all that I had lost, I could go into the HPC or head to class and get busy reclaiming my life.

That's exactly what I did. It meant everything for me to be able to go to a party, go to Witter Rugby Field for a match, or make new friends with my classmates. I didn't have to settle for FaceTime calls and watching live-streamed games on my computer. I could finally be in the action. It gave me a strong sense of progress and fulfillment.

While I was in the hospital, I never forgot what it felt like to watch others shape their lives. I would've given almost anything at that time to have my life back. As often as I could, I kept that perspective to help me realize every day at Cal was a gift that was not to be taken for granted. It was reflecting on the things that gave me joy that helped me work through my moments of despair.

Out of all the things that brought me happiness, the greatest was working out with Coach Billups.

Along with being the associate head coach, he runs the strength and conditioning program for the rugby team. Between him and Rachel Kahn, a great instructor who helped me with Neurokinetic Pilates, I was working out every day for at least an hour and a half. More importantly, I was almost always working out at the HPC, alongside the athletes I had trained with before my injury.

When I got hurt, Billups and Clark stood by me. On two occasions, they flew to Colorado to see me, and Billups started asking questions about my workouts when

I was there. He planned to help me with my rehab when I returned to school. He had no experience in spinal cord injury recovery, but he was going to continue to be my coach and help me perform at my best. I didn't even have to ask.

There was no one else I wanted to be in charge.

Beyond his advanced academic and real-world expertise in kinesiology, physiology, psychology, and anatomy, Billups started studying neuroscience and the intricacies of my rehab. He talked to my therapists and communicated with roughly a dozen experts in the Cal community. To me, it was truly one of the greatest gifts I've ever received.

To Billups, it was his duty. I'll let him explain.

> I'm Robert's coach, and I'll be his coach until they throw the last shovel of dirt on me. That relationship didn't end when he no longer played for us. I'm the one who pulled that jersey over his head and slapped him on the back to send him on his way the day he got hurt. I'm responsible for that. I'm responsible for him.
>
> Robert isn't the only player I've had who came back to us after he was done playing and needed help. He's different and he will be the most important coaching challenge of my life. Some of our guys need coaching down the road after a bump in the road and we're there for them. I think it's my purpose. I'm lucky to do what I'm supposed to be doing at a place where I can do it at the highest level. A lot of people don't get to live this kind of life.

When you have someone like that by your side, you can't help but want to run through any obstacle in front of you.

Every day presented a new challenge for me, and Billups helped me overcome each one of them. The training we did together healed my body and soul. We set goals and analyzed my progress together. He kept me pushing forward on the days when my body wasn't cooperating and helped me focus on reaching new heights when I was performing my best.

If my wheelchair broke and needed a repair, Billups was there to fix it. If it was raining and I needed help getting to a workout, Billups was at my door, jacket on and umbrella in hand, ready to push me up the hill. Here was one of the best rugby coaches the United States has ever produced helping me achieve my goals in ways completely outside of his job description.

Never have I seen someone so giving of their time and energy to a cause they didn't have an obligation to. I never would have been able to return to Cal and progress in my rehab if it weren't for Billups. The steps I take today are because of him.

Getting to work out with Billups was the highlight that pushed me through every difficult day. When we were training, all the stresses and hardships of life vanished. For a couple of hours each day, I could once again be an athlete with my coach, working to get better. He gave me my life back, and I am eternally grateful to him.

When I was at the HPC, I felt at home again. I felt normal again. If you're an athlete and you want to get pumped up, there's nothing better than the sound of heavy metal clanging on the weight machines or the thud of weights pounding the floor after a lift.

And as I worked out around my friends and former teammates, they would cheer me on.

"Way to go, Rob."

"Keep pushing, dude."

"Get after it, man."

I felt like part of the team again. If this was the closest thing I could get to my previous college life, I was going to reach for it with every last bit of energy in my body. In turn, I tried to do my part to inspire them. Billups agrees.

> In all probability, he gave as much to the other athletes as he got from them. You walk in there to train and maybe you're a little tired or not feeling great. Then you see Robert getting after it, busting his butt ten feet away from you. How are you going to complain? It was a poignant example. Robert did not ask for any quarter, nor was any quarter given. He's asking for a challenge.
>
> I can't begin to describe how it must have been for him to not be able to do what he was capable of doing before. It didn't matter. We'd just get busy doing what he needed to do. This is a guy who would light up a room and still can. He has that kind of energy and impact on people. You think about your own self-confidence and how it can be impacted by how we look or appear.
>
> Robert had every reason to not show up and work as hard as he did, and certainly not in front of fellow student-athletes who had seen him before. But that's not how he thinks and who he is. It's pretty much who he has always been. He was like that before he was injured, and the injury has made it more obvious and apparent for the world to see.

Nothing came without a challenge. There were moments when my body simply refused to cooperate. If that meant I urinated on myself, it was going to happen. There I was, training alongside some of the best athletes in college sports, and my body was betraying me like a two-year-old. Was it embarrassing? Sure. Was I going to let it stop me? Please. I didn't even think twice about it.

REFLECTION QUESTIONS

1. Think of a time in your past when something didn't go as planned. What are some of the ways you successfully adapted, and what are some things you wish you would've done differently?

2. What is something in your life right now that isn't going the way you planned? How can you reevaluate your plan to focus on the aspects within your control?

3. Who in your life can provide support and perspective as you navigate change or unmet expectations?

Chapter 12

BE A PART OF SOMETHING BIGGER THAN YOURSELF

Surround yourself with people who push you to do better and be better. No drama or negativity. Just higher goals and higher motivation...Simply bringing out the absolute best in each other.

—WARREN BUFFETT

COACH CLARK WAS apprehensive.

Years ago, a Cal Rugby player who had just graduated asked for a meeting with Clark. The player was a backup and didn't play in many of the big matches. The two sat in Clark's office with the door closed as Clark grew concerned that the player would want to vent about not having had more playing time.

"Coach, playing rugby at Cal has been the hardest thing I have ever done," the player started, Clark's heart sinking as he waited for the seemingly inevitable "but" and the unleashing of disappointment. The young man had invested hundreds upon hundreds of hours into the team. It's a reality of team sports, but it's nonetheless painful, and Clark owed it to the player to listen to his gripes.

"And I wouldn't trade it for anything," the player finished as the conversation turned in an unexpected direction.

All things considered, neither would I.

I share that view despite what happened to me. I wouldn't trade the opportunity to have played at Cal for anything, even the ability to walk again. What playing under Clark and Billups gave me was a much bigger lesson in what it takes to succeed in life. If you could give me back the use of my legs or full control of my arms, would I have the mental and physical toughness that came from playing for them?

Would I think "audaciously," as Billups describes it? Would I have the literal and figurative connections with people to make my audacious goals a reality?

To put it succinctly, would I live by the phrase "*Spectemur Agendo.*" That's the motto of Cal Rugby and loosely translates to "to be known by your deeds." It is about what you do with your life, not what you say.

I know this: I don't think I would have been able to handle the challenges I have faced without being part of this team. That starts with surviving and extends to graduating. I wouldn't have made it through without the help of my rugby teammates, coaches, and staff. From taking out the trash to doing laundry to getting around campus to fighting through the mental hardships, I needed every bit of "air cover," as Clark and Billups like to call it.

I needed the deeds of my teammates.

I also don't want to suggest that the benefits of being part of something larger than yourself are exclusive to Cal Rugby.

I realize that some of you read my description and think, "That's great for you, Robert, but I'm not a rugby player, and I didn't go to a school like Cal." Fair point. My response is that while the school and its rugby team are a unique combination of athletic and academic excellence, that mission-based focus doesn't stand alone at Cal.

There are many organizations out there with purpose and history. The United States military, the Salvation Army, and Kiwanis are among the many. There were clubs and organizations I was involved with in high school and college. Cal Rugby happened to be the one that lined up best with my values and skills. It ignited my passion and then fed my recovery.

My overarching point is this: Be part of something larger than yourself. Whatever it is, contribute to it. Give all you can to it. Hold yourself to its legacy and great standards, and do everything in your power to raise the level of the group and those within it. That was the real value I got from playing rugby at Cal. While I went there with the intent of being an exceptional athlete and getting a great education, my experience with Cal Rugby gave me more than I could ever imagine.

It gave me the ability to touch other people's lives. I learned both the cost of success and the importance of sacrifice. It's part of a legacy that has grown for more than a century and has been taken to the highest level by Clark and Billups.

A CULTURE OF EXCELLENCE

Over the past forty years, Cal has set the standard for success in American collegiate rugby. It is like the Alabama football or Duke basketball of American rugby, a brand with a history of title expectation.

Many people involved in American rugby take it a step further, comparing Cal Rugby's dominance to the famous New Zealand All Blacks national team. The All Blacks are one of the winningest rugby organizations in international history.

When you add on the fact that Cal is one of the greatest universities in the United States and widely recognized as one of the world's leading public educational institutions, you have two drawing cards that are incredibly attractive to any serious teenage rugby player. In high school, all I wanted was to go to Cal and play rugby. Every other school that talked to me was a distant second.

I came in expecting to grow as a rugby player and student. Then I was introduced to the culture.

That culture has been built by generations of young men striving for excellence since the program's inception in 1882 as Cal's first intercollegiate sport. At the time of writing this book, its record of success includes 11 Olympians, 157 All-Americans, and 60 players who have made 761 combined appearances on the United States National 15s Team. Since 1980, the team has won a total of thirty-three national championships, and the program has only had six head coaches in its 140-plus years of competition.

You can't help but feel humbled to be a part of a team of such caliber. That history feeds the larger goal of what Clark and Billups are continuously working to improve. The offices of the program are reflective of that dedication to the program's roots.

Clark and Billups took a small building that used to be a men's bathroom next to an old, muddy field along the east rim of Cal's Memorial Stadium and transformed it into a respected place of history. The wood-paneled field house is not just a shrine to the Cal program, but to the game itself. Nearly one hundred photos and framed artifacts, including a jersey from the 1924 gold medal-winning USA Olympic team, cover almost every inch of the walls like mosaic tiles.

When you walk in, the phrase *Spectemur Agendo* is directly above the door to the main room of the field house. This isn't like some locker room with cheesy inspirational phrases all over the place. This is a place where the deeds of the men who came before us are chronicled.

There are plenty of trophies on display, but they are secondary to the photos of the players and the memories they forged. Next to the field house is Witter Rugby Field. The mud and muck are long gone, replaced by an immaculate synthetic surface and pristine lines that map the rugby-dedicated field.

When you become part of that program, the standard is to compete for championships. However, I found that winning championships is a by-product of something larger and more intricately evolved. The core mission is to shape men of character. Rugby is a vehicle by which that goal is accomplished. What Clark and Billups are doing with the players is an extension of both their personal motivation and their sense of duty to those who came before them.

This motivation has produced an exceptional level of success for its student-athletes, both on and off the field. Cal Rugby has long been a training ground for men who eventually become successful as professionals once their playing days are over. In turn, it's very common to give back to the program and support the next generation of Golden Bears.

Philanthropy within Cal Rugby is legendary. The program has always been and continues to be self-supporting, with no financial support from the university's intercollegiate athletics department. The total endowment for the team exceeds $25 million, in addition to robust annual funding, raising on average several hundred thousand dollars a year for the program's annual account.

In 2018 alone, the rugby community showed its ongoing support by establishing eight new positional endowments for $250,000 each. Since then, additional positional endowments have been created. The program has numerous endowments, but only fifteen positional endowments, one for each position on the rugby team. Once a positional endowment is filled, it is filled for life, so to have your name permanently connected to the program's philanthropy is a rarefied, highly exclusive honor.

I was incredibly fortunate to have an endowment named in my honor for the lock position, funded by Byron Deeter. At twenty-five years old, Deeter founded Trigo Technologies, which was acquired by IBM while preparing for an IPO in 2004. Now, he is a partner at Bessemer Venture Partners, with twenty-six of his investments currently valued above $1 billion, including a dozen IPOs and counting. As a player at Cal, he was a starting front-row player for the Golden Bears in the 1990s and a four-time national champion. To say he's an exemplary man would be a massive understatement.

It's most common for endowments to be named in honor of the donor or their family, but it's not uncommon in Cal Rugby to give in the name of others. Deeter generously chose the title of The Robert J. Paylor Rugby Lock Endowment. To be recognized by him will always be one of the greatest honors I have ever received. "Robert will always have a place among those fifteen," Deeter said. "Like many others, I have been inspired by him. Reflecting on what Cal Rugby meant to me, its impact on making me the person I am now, the budgetary challenges of the university, and the goals of the program, I was moved to make this gift."

The history of success with people such as Deeter and

many other benefactors defines a big part of Cal Rugby's impact on the men who played. It harkens to the young man who told Clark about how important rugby was to his college experience even though he didn't play much. "One after another, you hear the former players say Cal Rugby is the hardest thing they did in college and they don't want it to change," Billups says. "And then they slide that check across the table...It's not supposed to be easy. We're not doing this for recreation. We're not just doing this for fun. We're doing this to provide all our student-athletes a really rich, heartfelt experience of setting an audacious goal and working our tails off to try to achieve it."

I couldn't agree more.

While I came to Cal expecting to graduate as the best rugby player I could be, I left as the best person I could be. During my two years playing rugby at Cal, I gained invaluable principles that I have applied daily since. This program laid the foundation that allowed me to respond constructively to my injury, starting from day one.

At Cal, we're not taught to accept mediocrity collectively as a team or individually as players. Our expectation year in and year out is to be the best, and not just the best team in the nation, but the best version of ourselves.

In our postgame review sessions, whether we won or lost, Clark would start off the meeting by asking what we did well. A player would raise their hand and share an aspect of the game that they found to be one of our strengths, and a collaborative discussion would ensue where other players would offer reasons why they agreed or not. Each explanation was backed by statistics and specific moments in the game to support their reasoning. Once there was a consensus, a scribe would write the area of strength on the whiteboard, and the process would continue.

Eventually, we would shift our focus to areas of the game that did not go well. We used the same collaborative process to create a list of areas for improvement. These assessments guided our training and how we prepared for future matches.

If an outsider were to observe these meetings, they wouldn't know whether we won or lost and by how much. Our focus was on our performance—how we could leverage our strengths and address our shortcomings.

I've approached my rehabilitation the same way we approached our postgame analysis. I look for small victories, no matter how minor they seem, and celebrate them. I evaluate my setbacks with the same collaborative spirit, seeking input from my doctors, therapists, and loved ones to understand how to adjust my focus and how to improve.

This relentless pursuit of growth and the ability to critically analyze both successes and failures have been invaluable in my journey. Just as we did on the rugby field, I learned to measure my progress not by immediate outcomes, but by the effort and dedication I put into each step of the recovery process.

This is one of many examples of the lessons that have served me long after I last stepped foot on the field. It isn't the rugby skills that serve me through my post-sports endeavors; it's life skills such as mental toughness, selflessness, leadership, and other core values of Cal Rugby. These aren't things that I could have taught myself. It's the culmination of more than a century of young men striving for excellence that molded me into the person I am today.

And there are not many people who are as inspiring as someone who helped our nation in one of its darkest moments.

THE BINGHAM STANDARD

While I like to think my story embodies the spirit of Cal Rugby and that I did everything I could to live up to the standards set before me, I'm in a long line of people who have turned their Cal Rugby experience into personal and professional success.

At the front of that line is the story of Mark Bingham.

Bingham grew up in Los Gatos, California, and fell in love with the sport in high school. He loved to smile and was a great teammate with his infectious enthusiasm and unwavering support both on and off the field.

Bingham wasn't a star at Cal, but he played at a critical time in the development of the program. He was part of the 1991 national championship team that set the stage for an extended run of dominance unmatched by any other school since.

Bingham leveraged his experience in Berkeley to build an incredibly successful life. He started his own public relations firm in San Francisco and later expanded to New York City. He also joined the San Francisco Fog rugby team. By age thirty-one, he had positioned himself for a great life and career.

Then, Bingham made the ultimate sacrifice. On September 11, 2001, he was on United Airlines Flight 93 from Newark International Airport to San Francisco. After the plane was hijacked by terrorists and it became clear it would be used as part of an attack on the United States, Bingham and the other passengers devised a plan to confront the knife-wielding terrorists.

They fought to regain control of the plane and, if nothing else, ensure it didn't crash into a target, as three other planes did that day, bringing down the World Trade

Center buildings and damaging the Pentagon. Many believe that Flight 93 was bound for Washington, DC, targeting the Capitol Building while Congress was in session.

Instead, Flight 93 crashed into a field in rural Pennsylvania. No one survived.

Shortly after, the late Senator John McCain offered a eulogy at a memorial service for Bingham. "I may very well owe my life to Mark," said the naval aviator, former prisoner of war, congressman, senator, and presidential candidate. McCain's eulogy for Bingham continued:

> I never knew Mark Bingham. But I wish I had. I know he was a good son and friend, a good rugby player, a good American and an extraordinary human being. He supported me, and his support now ranks among the greatest honors of my life. I wish I had known before September 11 just how great an honor his trust in me was. I wish I could have thanked him for it more profusely than time and circumstances allowed. But I know it now. And I thank him with the only means I possess, by being as good an American as he was.

Bingham and the other passengers who stormed the cockpit are heroes. They are the true definition of the word.

I know my struggle and everything Cal Rugby helped me overcome. I can only imagine the fear that Bingham and the others must have conquered, surely knowing that their attempt to regain control of the plane would be their final hour.

That's a willingness to be part of something truly greater than oneself. That's truly audacious.

Throughout each challenge I face, I have someone to look up to in the Cal Rugby program for inspiration and guidance. Whether through the professional success of many alumni or the ultimate display of heroism and courage by Bingham, the standard set by those before me provides every example I need of how I ought to live.

To think that I wore the same colors and shared the same goal as those great men is both humbling and motivating. Having that standard to live up to pushes me to perform better, hoping to continue promoting those values.

A COMMITMENT TO GET BETTER

Yes, Cal Rugby gets great players.

Yes, Cal Rugby has a top-notch training facility.

Yes, Cal Rugby is better self-funded than most collegiate rugby programs.

That doesn't mean that playing for Cal is easy or that success isn't earned each year through hard work. Just ask someone who once played against us, served as a coaching intern under Billups, and has watched the program for more than twenty years.

"It's the work ethic," says Patrick Culley, a former rugby player who sustained a paralyzing injury in 2004. Culley played at Humboldt State in Northern California and continued on the national club circuit before being injured. "When I played in college, we always used to complain that Cal got the best players, and they had the money to have a weight room and whatever else. A lot of that is true. But the foundation is that they get after it. There's no complacency. They target individuals who can handle the demands of what they are asking, both from a training and a class-load standpoint. They're practicing six days a week and working out seven. That's not just about talent. That's work."

Clark and Billups approach recruiting differently than most. It's about finding a "match," not just convincing someone to join the team. Will the athlete fit into the culture and make the necessary sacrifices? Does he have the right mindset to play for Cal? Can he handle the academic rigor of the university? They are careful to study people beyond just athletic talent.

Or as Clark has referred to it, it's the old saying from famed college football coach Bo Schembechler, which basically says that if you miss on a great recruit who goes to another team, he might beat you only once a year. On the other hand, if you recruit the wrong player to your team, he's going to beat you every day.

"We had our program, and we thought we could compete with them by practicing twice a week," Culley said. "Then I started to realize, 'Hey, why don't we do what they're doing? Why don't we get after it the same way they do?'... Clark is a unique character who elevated that program, no doubt, and he has a perfect complement in Billups and how they run the program together. Between the tradition of the program and the organizational expertise that Clark used to raise the program to the highest level possible, there is a sense of duty."

Or as Jack Clark's Cal Rugby mindset states: "Grateful for everything, entitled to nothing."

As a rugby player at Cal, you don't take for granted that someone washes your equipment or uniform for you. You're grateful for that. You appreciate it. You don't need a pristine field to warm up on before a match. You'll warm up in a parking garage if you have to.

There's a mindset that nothing is owed to you. You work for what you have. I relied on this approach daily in my recovery.

I proceeded with the expectation that the journey to walking again wasn't going to just happen. It had to be earned through a daily commitment to improve. It was ingrained in me that there is no backing down from the challenge. Or as Clark and Billups preach, live by the value of "constant performance improvement."

It's the mentality that every day is an opportunity to get better, and if you're working hard at something, you need to demonstrate improvement. It drives Cal's rugby players to put in the work, not just rely on talent. When I was at Cal, I knew I had the size and athletic ability to make the team. But that didn't nearly cut it to break into the starting lineup.

I had to push myself to physical extremes like the times I worked out until I threw up. I knew it wasn't enough to just work out during the season or our scheduled practices, and I could see the improvements that went with pushing myself.

That was one sense of satisfaction. I also lived for the moments when Clark would say, "Attaboy." When Clark talked about me earning a starting job as a sophomore, I was over the moon.

There was also the flip side, which I did everything to avoid. There was a time Clark said during a day-after-game review, "Paylor, you owe us ten dollars for a ticket from yesterday. All you did was show up and watch." That's a heck of a line. I deserved it.

Cal Rugby is built around the precept of chasing greatness through collective struggle. People who are willing to work together through strain and sacrifice. As a result, you feel equipped to handle any challenge, be it physical or mental.

And when I say any challenge, I mean even the

preposterous ones we like to imagine. Clark likes to say that you could drop a group of us in a city we've never been to, naked, with no money, and no plan. By the end of the day, we'll have clothes on our backs, some money in our pockets, and a plan. That's the Cal Rugby ethos in action. That's what I strive to live up to.

THE COLLECTIVE SPIRIT

While some may find that last hypothetical absurd—or know that it's one used by some other groups, particularly the military—I know my example. I was left paralyzed, face down on a field with all sorts of adversity ahead of me.

But I wasn't alone, and that was critical.

I had my family, friends, and the support of my Cal Rugby brethren. Clark, Billups, and my teammates were there practically every day. Danny Barrett, who is a two-time Olympian and one of the greatest players in Cal history, flew in from Portland to check on me in the first month. His presence and care were an immense boost to my morale.

It's part of the connection we have with each other.

"I get calls from guys who played before me and guys who played after me," Barrett says. "It doesn't matter how old you are or when you played. If you played rugby at Cal, people know what you're about and what you're made of."

It's a bond that has carried other men to great personal and financial success. It's a bond that helped one man become a hero during our country's darkest moment.

It's a bond that is priceless.

While I was elated to return to Cal after my injury, I was scared too. Everywhere I went, I had a mountain to climb...literally.

Berkeley's geography is much like San Francisco's. It's hills for days. Even my scooter sometimes struggled to lug my body through the streets of Berkeley before my injury. Those hills could give even Lance Armstrong a run for his money.

As the fall semester of 2018 approached, my coaches put together a spreadsheet listing all the times when I needed to get to and from classes and workouts, or when I needed help with a task, such as taking out the garbage or doing laundry. One by one, Cal Rugby players, coaches, and staff signed up to help. Most times, I had three or four teammates by my side as we navigated campus.

Whether I was lacing up my cleats or not, it was clear that I would always be a part of the team. It's the kind of program where if you fall, there will be an army of people behind you to pick you up and carry you forward.

I can't begin to explain how much that meant to me. Everything about life had become exponentially harder. Doing laundry wouldn't seem that difficult to most. Try getting through the gate to the laundry room in a wheelchair. I couldn't do it by myself. Same thing with taking out the garbage.

The support went beyond just completing daily tasks. It showed me I was never alone. I didn't have to start over and go through college by myself when I returned to Berkeley, and I didn't even have to ask to be included in team activities. I was still part of something meaningful, and if I ever needed anything, I knew I had people I could count on.

Frankly, I wouldn't have graduated if it weren't for the rugby team.

While the term "Cal Rugby man" carries its own sense of significance—complete with stories and shared experiences that thousands of former players understand with a nod—the basic concept is not unique.

Whatever meaningful organization it is, there's a debt we owe to those who came before us that we pay for those who come after us. When you become part of a program that has reached that level of greatness, you don't want to let down either those before you or those who come after you. You don't want to be the one who let the standard of excellence slip.

And when you give to the program, they wrap their arms around you and protect you in your time of need. Cal Rugby had my back the entire way.

REFLECTION QUESTIONS

1. As you think about your current goals and challenges, are you surrounded by people and mentors who inspire you, challenge you, and support your growth?

2. Who are the organizations or groups you admire most in your life, and what values or traits do they represent that you wish to embody?

3. What goals do you have for the groups you're a part of, beyond just your own personal goals? What can you do to make those goals a reality?

Chapter 13

SEE THE GIFT OF CHALLENGES

I met Robert for the first time maybe two or three days after he was hurt. Here he was, fighting pneumonia, trying to recover from surgery, and lying there paralyzed. The nurses and doctors are pounding on his chest trying to get him to cough up phlegm, he's on monitors, lying there motionless and he's talking to me about how he's going to get into the Haas School of Business and take my class. I went home that night and told my wife, "I don't think he's going to survive." Maybe eighteen months later, there he is, sitting in front of my class with this big smile on his face.

—SOLLY FULP, PROFESSOR AT HAAS SCHOOL OF BUSINESS

I FELT THE POWER of silence. I sat in my wheelchair and opened my heart about the challenges I faced and the odds I had overcome to be back at Cal. I was sharing my testimony with fellow students in Professor Solly Fulp's class. Fulp had asked me to share my story, and I poured everything I had into this presentation.

I was lighthearted at first to engage the audience and then build the drama. Then it happened. I paused for a moment during my twenty-minute talk as silence overtook the room. It was so quiet that if a pin had dropped, it would have sounded like a cymbal being clanged.

I had never felt that kind of power. I had felt the strength of moving people in the past, but it came with grunts and the sounds of bodies colliding amid the aggressive chatter of a rugby game. I took immense pride in the ability to move people as an athlete. This was a different level of satisfaction.

In sports, moving people is about competition. It's about overwhelming an opponent in an effort to make them submit, quit, and accept defeat. It's a zero-sum activity where only one side comes out victorious. I loved that competition, and there are an immense number of benefits to sports.

Yet it's not the same as raising the spirits of a group of people, each with their own challenges. Or maybe I'm giving them a blueprint for achieving their goals, spurring hope that guides or inspires them to push forward.

That is true power. Sitting in front of my peers at that moment, that power coursed through my body. It filled me with something more profound than the ability to walk, run, or win a big game. That's when I first realized that through all of this pain and suffering, I had been given a gift. In the process of losing so much of my previous identity, I gained a new ability that I could share with others.

And I wouldn't trade that by wishing my injury had never happened.

People hear me say that and they probably think I'm either a liar or a lunatic. Coach Clark and my co-writer, Jason Cole, have separately advised me that I shouldn't say that. It's hard to imagine anyone would truly not wish away an injury like mine.

I listened to Clark and Cole candidly and took in their perspectives, but it's difficult to fully understand where I'm coming from. To be honest, I'm not sure very many people can. Nobody has experienced every second of my life as I have. Likewise, Cole once asked me if I was saying it as a way of coming to terms with my injury.

I say it because it's my truth. I don't say it because it sounds profound or because I'm trying to spin a cliché or convince myself. Through the experiences I've had, the people I've met, and the selfless purpose this injury has given me, how could I possibly wish that away?

But I do want to explain myself a bit. Yes, I want to regain my ability to walk again and have my full independence back. I work at that in my rehab every day. What I don't want is to wish this injury had never happened in the first place.

Changing what happened to me would mean wishing away relationships with people like Talon Bonanno, experiences like I had in Lourdes, and an ability to help others through adversity at a level I don't think I would've gained without this injury. I love my life, and I'm proud of where I am today. If my past is the road I had to take to inspire people in this way, then I'm grateful for it.

I used to be able to move people through brute force. Now, I move their minds, hearts, and souls. It's more meaningful than anything I could have imagined before May 6, 2017, or in the days, weeks, and months that followed.

Finding the gift in challenges is difficult to see when in the middle of hardship. Adversity can come with seasons of suffering and despair, and in some cases, lives can feel completely upended. When dealing with the immediacy of a challenge, most people don't have the time or desire to think about what positives are coming out of the situation.

However, to fully heal, I find it necessary to see our gifts, those things that we have retained and gained. Nearly everyone has heard, "When one door closes, another opens" or "Smooth seas don't make skillful sailors." While these sayings can feel like overused clichés, I think there is truth to the essence of the shared message. Challenges and setbacks can lead to positive outcomes or personal growth if approached with the right mindset. By choosing to persevere, one can gain resilience, an appreciation for simple joys, and an ability to empathize with and serve others in a way that is heightened through hardship.

I understand that this can be a difficult concept to embrace. If someone had sat beside me on the first day after my injury and tried to convince me there were positives to being paralyzed, I would've asked security to escort them out of my room. I was fighting for my life while battling the fear of how much had changed and the limits of my future. I would've thought, "How could anything good possibly come from this?"

After everything I've been through and the persistence I've put forward, I can honestly say that the positives of this journey outweigh the negatives. The fortitude and perspective I've gained, the relationships I've built, and the selfless purpose I've been granted amount to more than all of the suffering I've endured.

Through the force of what has happened and how I have pushed myself, I have discovered a power within me that I never really recognized. I suppose it was always there, hidden beneath the surface as I focused on developing the raw, external power and energy that allowed me to be a part of an elite athletic program.

That power would come out in glimpses, such as helping Talon feel included at the Jesuit High School youth rugby camp or serving the Blackfeet Indian Tribe in Montana. But it wasn't the focal point of my existence. It wasn't the objective that I decided to turn into my purpose.

When I found what that power and strength could do for others, it created a sense of meaning more powerful than anything I ever did on the rugby pitch or in any other sporting event I could have imagined.

Simply put, that moment of silence was addicting.

It happened shortly after I returned to Cal in 2018. As the quote that precedes this chapter indicates, I didn't meet Fulp until a few days after my injury. I knew of him through family friends and people at Cal who had taken his class. I had always hoped to take his class, and I told him that as he watched me struggle to survive. I laid out my plan to return to Cal in one year and shared my goals with him while enduring the most incredible duress.

When I returned to Cal, I met with Fulp for coffee at the Haas School of Business. As we talked about everything I had been through and the excitement of returning to campus, he told me that he wanted me to speak to his class.

He had students who were dealing with an array of problems that were holding them back. They weren't visual problems like mine. One student was dealing with the death of a close friend in a car accident. Another had a close family member who was very sick. Many students confided in Fulp about their various troubles.

These people were struggling in the shadows. They didn't have a wheelchair that showed they needed help or that they were hurt. There was no one running up to help them.

And even the people who didn't have difficult life challenges had goals and aspirations they wanted to achieve. They had desires to graduate, have great careers, and perform to their highest potential. Even though these aren't challenges like overcoming an injury or the loss of a loved one, the approach to achieving those goals is highly translatable.

Fulp knew that I had the potential to share my experiences and inspire others. I immediately and excitedly accepted the offer. We set the date for October 22, and I went to Clark for help.

Not surprisingly, Clark is a highly sought-after keynote speaker. He's famous for his ability to speak and consult on organizational culture, leadership, and high performance. With those skills combined with his immense care and interest in my success, there was no one else I would rather have by my side.

Clark and I discussed some ideas and promised to reconvene to refine my thoughts. From there, I went back to my apartment and started to think about all the things that had helped me overcome my injury. I thought about the mental tools that included controlling my mindset, practicing perspective, and feeding myself a positive mental diet, and I poured it all out on paper.

Then, I started putting together a list of stories about how those tools shaped my life and could help others. I met with Clark again and started matching the tools with the appropriate stories or thinking of where we could incorporate some outside source material.

The goal was to deliver a twenty-minute speech, which I had never done before. I had ample material through my experiences. At the same time, I wanted to make it relatable. Everyone has a unique challenge, and I wanted people to think about the potential they possessed to overcome what they faced.

After Clark and I developed a framework for the message, I wrote my first speech. I started by introducing the topic of human performance. I detailed the buildup and aftermath of when I was injured in 2017, and I explained how I dealt with the short-term and long-term challenges. Then I laid out the tools that help me overcome my hardships and how they can help others accomplish their goals. Clark and I revised my speech numerous times, and I practiced again and again. I just wasn't quite sure how the audience was going to react.

I had never poured my soul out to people like this. As a leader in retreats, at school, or in sports, I had given my fair share of talks. The typical speech lasted for a few minutes in front of fellow students, parents, teachers, and administrators. I had given plenty of pep talks to teammates in practices, before games, or at halftime. But those were maybe a minute or two, if that.

This was a whole new level of opening up and engaging the audience for twenty minutes. I practiced for hours in front of a mirror, but I didn't know how it would go. One way or another, on October 22, 2018, it was time for me to step up.

I sat in front of the class on the fifth floor of Chou Hall in the Haas School of Business. I remember having those butterflies like I used to get before games. Clark gave me an amazing introduction that amped my motivation. I scanned the room of roughly fifty students, almost all of them juniors and seniors. Their desks were arranged in an inverted-U shape in front of me. I didn't have a microphone. I just projected my voice.

I had my notes in my lap, and I relied on them at first. Then I started to get more and more comfortable. I could feel the connection developing. They were engaged. I told the story about how I sometimes tell little kids that I got paralyzed from not eating vegetables. Everybody cracked up.

I continued talking about my life before my injury. Again, it was lighthearted and joyful because that's how my life had been up to that moment. I described getting to the day of my injury and how I was living out my dream. I talked about getting ready for the game, riding the bus, and putting on my jersey. Everybody laughed or smiled at the right times.

Then I started describing the early moments of the game, breaking down how the maul developed and collapsed. As I finished the description, I said, "I closed my eyes, gritted my teeth, and then snap!" While I was describing the moment, I showed a photo of me in the headlock. As I said "snap," the photo switched to a sideline view of me with my face hitting my chest as I hit the ground and my neck broke.

That's when I paused and let the quiet of the moment speak for me. The audience was captivated.

As the speech went on, I could hear and see people crying. No one was peeking at their cell phone or opening a laptop. When I finished, the students rose for a standing ovation and then approached me to shake my hand. Some shared their struggles or told me how my story had inspired them. Some were still crying.

I beamed with joy at the thought that I had touched and inspired so many people. Both Fulp and Clark told me how well it had gone. Each of them said, "Robert, you know, this could be something you do for a living." I had never thought about being a public speaker, but I was immediately enamored with the idea.

I went back to my apartment and all I could think was, "When am I going to speak again?" I was hooked on the rush of knowing I could do something good for others by sharing this message.

I was fortunate enough to get more opportunities to speak, the next time with Intel, the company where I had been an intern. Specifically, the Intel operations group wanted me to speak because it was dealing with supply chain challenges. I went to the Folsom campus, just outside of Sacramento, and spoke to roughly 250 people in person and a total of maybe 300 over a video feed. I altered the speech for a business crowd and Intel's specific situation, but the core message was the same.

Again, I had my doubts about what to expect. This wasn't a group of students. I was speaking to seasoned, sophisticated businesspeople. These are people who have already dealt with elaborate problems in their lives. It's also not often that the intern gives advice to their managers.

And once again, the power of that silent moment took hold. As the speech went on, they laughed, they cried, and all rose for a standing ovation. Afterward, a line of employees approached me or sent messages about how deeply my presentation had moved them.

I imagine this must be what it feels like for a great singer or artist to discover their true calling. Or when a great lawyer presents a case in front of the Supreme Court and captivates the justices. Or maybe when a leader delivers a speech that rallies the people.

All I knew was that I had found my calling.

And I mean calling in the truest sense of the word. This wasn't some fallback plan, even if it wasn't the future I had imagined. While my rugby career ended prematurely, that was never really the long-term plan. I had it in my mind that I would work for a company like Intel and strive for a career as a business executive.

Instead, I now had a purpose I was driven to pursue above all else. I was enraptured by the idea of speaking, and I decided to dedicate my life to it. Out of this challenge was born a gift, and that's a gift I can give to others.

REFLECTION QUESTIONS

1. What are some gifts you've discovered through difficult times? What are the lessons you learned, relationships you built, and new opportunities that opened up?

2. In what area of your life can you stop focusing on the immediate outcome and instead commit to the long-term growth you can gain from pushing forward?

3. Are there ways in which you can help others going through similar challenges as you?

Chapter 14
KNOW YOU'RE WORTHY OF LOVE

Everyone in the world should get a standing ovation at least
once in their life because we all overcometh the world.

—R. J. PALACIO, *WONDER*

I FELT THE ADULATION of ten thousand and the love of
one.

We all crave a sense of worthiness, whether it comes
from a standing ovation or a simple text from someone we
care about.

Knowing you're loved is as essential as food and water.
We can't live without it. Nothing important is accomplished alone, and there is not a moment I've spent without
having people in this world who care about me.

It's one of the blessings I'm most grateful for in my
life, because I'm well aware that not everyone receives
this same kind of attention. Remembering this fuels my
commitment to extend kindness and support to others,
because everyone deserves to feel seen and valued.

In sharing my journey, I've been so fortunate to receive
reminders of how kind others can be. Sometimes they
send me a message. Sometimes they stop me if we cross
paths in public. Sometimes they even stand up to cheer,
smile, and cry all at once, the way nearly ten thousand

family, friends, professors, administrators, and classmates did at the graduation for the Cal Class of 2020.

That happened on August 29, 2021, at the Greek Theatre in Berkeley, which is a beautiful outdoor amphitheater. It's among the most hallowed ground at Cal, hosting legendary artists in the past like the Beatles and Bob Dylan, and iconic leaders such as Martin Luther King Jr., President Franklin D. Roosevelt, and Winston Churchill.

My class at Cal had to wait a year to walk for our diplomas because of COVID-19. It's about eight or nine steps from the moment you hear your name called to where you stop to get your diploma. Most celebrated with a casual walk across the stage after their name was announced. A few people added some strut or even a dance move. One classmate pretended as if he were dribbling a basketball between his legs.

Then there was one classmate dressed in a pink cap and gown. As she crossed, she did a cartwheel. If Mary Kay Cosmetics gave pink airplanes instead of pink Cadillacs as prizes for their salespeople, this girl could have been a propeller. She was awesome.

But of all the people who walked across the stage, I was the one who brought people to their feet because that's exactly how I received my degree.

Standing up.

Better yet, I had my girlfriend (and now wife), Karsen Welle, at my side.

This was a moment I dreamed and prayed about for years. When I needed inspiration during lonely nights or grueling workouts, I thought of how amazing it would be to one day graduate and receive my diploma on my feet. Four years earlier, I was told this accomplishment would never come. Now, this vision was becoming my reality.

Even though standing up and making those steps was an easy feat in my routine workouts, it's different when there are ten thousand people focused solely on you. I sat among my classmates in the bowl of the Greek Theatre, scanning the faces of thousands of people. I felt the same butterflies I used to get before a rugby match.

Eventually, I rolled my way to the stage and prepared to do what I had dreamed of for so long. My nerves were at their peak. I was next up to be called, so as we had practiced, Coach Billups crouched in front of me and stabilized my walker as I shot my legs forward to get ready. I gripped my walker, dug my feet into the ground, and made the slow rise to stand tall. As if on cue, the crowd stood and filled the Greek Theatre with a roar of applause as I made the trek of those eight or nine steps with the help of Billups and Karsen.

I turned to face the crowd, Billups handed me my diploma, and I thrust it into the air with a beaming grin. As I listened to the cheers from family, friends, classmates, and strangers, I experienced one of the proudest moments of my life. Some people who didn't even know me wept as I stood there. The outpouring of love from everyone there was something I will never forget.

I hope that when people saw me walk across the stage, they saw themselves overcoming their own challenges. I was told it would be an accomplishment to feed myself again one day. Here I was receiving my diploma on my feet.

And doing it next to the woman I love.

Returning to Cal wasn't only about earning my degree. There were other goals to set and questions to answer. Would I have a purpose? Would I have a successful job?

I also wondered if I would be worthy of being loved in

a romantic way, not just by my family and closest friends. To experience that kind of love, you also must learn to love yourself. That wasn't easy for me to do.

The month I spent bedridden and hardly able to eat punished my body. After losing sixty pounds, my once athletic body atrophied away as I could see the ridges in my sternum and rib cage. I looked in the mirror and saw a body I didn't recognize. I thought I was unworthy of love. That's a horrible feeling.

It wasn't just the physical aspect that worried me, but the challenges that my partner would have to face. I can't just take a spontaneous trip when I have a free weekend. It's arduous and takes planning. I don't get to do a lot of things that are just spur of the moment. There are logistical hurdles and cancellations.

That's just one example of the day-to-day hardships. In the grander scale of life, there are much more delicate and far-reaching issues, such as life expectancy and having children.

One of the things that most people don't realize is that my accident shortened my life expectancy by roughly twenty years. It's a harsh reality that I don't like thinking about. But when you can't exercise, your body deteriorates, and there's a long list of medical complications that come with paralysis. I work every day to improve my health, but I'm fighting against harrowing odds.

As for having children, there are a lot of questions my partner and I have to maneuver, ranging from infertility issues to adoption. These are intensely private issues that would be a burden for any couple.

I was thinking, "In what world does an attractive, smart, successful, and athletic woman in her twenties sign up to marry a guy like me who makes life harder on a daily basis, who has medical issues starting a family, and, finally, might not be around in old age?"

Being with me requires effort and sacrifice, and not everyone is willing to take that on. But Karsen is.

The funny part of our story is that I didn't pick up on the clues at first.

The first time I met Karsen was in the fall of 2019. I was invited to an Athletes in Action meeting, which is called AIA for short. AIA is a group for Christian athletes. Karsen and I had a mutual friend named Caihla who was going. Caihla convinced me to go and helped walk me to the meeting. When Caihla came over, Karsen was with her. Karsen was on the club volleyball team at the time and was a member of AIA.

I thought Karsen was beautiful, so I was my outgoing self and tried to strike up a conversation with her. Initially, I thought my effort was a swing and a miss. I thought she wasn't interested in the least bit, which was not altogether surprising given the way I thought about my condition. When you have based so much of your self-image on being an athlete and your physical abilities, it's hard to make an immediate transition in your head about how people view and appreciate you.

That's a complicated way of saying that I totally misread the situation. It turned out that she was interested in me as much as I was interested in her. Unlike me, Karsen is a little more reserved. Lucky for me, one of Karsen's friends was dating one of my best friends, Chase Bixby. A few months later, I was talking to Chase about Karsen, and he basically told me, "Hey, idiot. She really likes you!"

We set up a double date, and because I had come to my senses, we totally hit it off. I saw she was funny, driven, and athletic; we shared the same values, and she was downright beautiful. To top it off, she worked as a care-giver for a woman with cerebral palsy in Berkeley, so she understood much of what it's like to live with a disability. She was everything I had prayed for.

What I found in Karsen was someone who embodied everything I hoped for in a life partner. The quality of the person she is makes sense when you learn how great her family is too.

Karsen is the second-oldest child of a father who is an orthopedic surgeon and a mother who was an ob-gyn. Her mother's ability to perform surgeries became more diffi-cult after a bike accident caused her to lose some function in one hand.

Her mother's answer was to go to law school and become a lawyer. Yeah, they're kind of high-achieving people. Karsen was raised with both the compassion of doctors and the drive of three doctorates. You put all of that together and it makes an impressive person.

To say I was captivated by her would be an understate-ment. From there, we did almost everything together. We'd study, go to sports events, travel, go to church, and celebrate each other's victories like they were our own. Each experience brought us closer together and strength-ened our bond.

Karsen helped me see my life not in terms of limita-tions, but possibilities. What I couldn't do for myself, she did for me, and she did it with joy. Her unwavering sup-port showed me that being paralyzed had nothing to do with my worth. It's who I was inside that deserved her love.

Of course, our friends and family sensed our com-mitment to each other, and soon, the proposal questions began.

"Robert, are you going to ask her soon?" was one version.

"So, Robert, what are your plans?" was another version of the question.

Then, of course, came the remarks from my closest buddies who took no shame in reminding me that Karsen and I had been dating since March 2019.

"Dude, you better ask her before she wises up and drops you," my buddies would say, reminding me of the idea that with friends like this, you needn't concern yourself with foes. All kidding aside, it's also hard to propose when that person is your ride everywhere.

We went ring shopping in November 2022, and I had the ring for a while. Again, I'm getting all the questions at this point. There was just one problem: I couldn't figure out how to meet with Karsen's parents to ask for their blessing without her finding out. I wasn't driving at the time, so pretty much whenever I was near her folks, it was because she drove me to them.

I couldn't invite them to lunch on the sly to ask them for her hand without asking Karsen, "Hey, honey, could you drive me to Santa Cruz so I can get lunch with your parents?" Kind of a dead giveaway. But one day in December 2022, we were at their house and Karsen was sleeping in. I got up a little early and went looking for Dr. Tom and Dana Welle.

Her dad was just getting out of the hot tub, which wasn't an ideal opportunity to ask your future in-laws this type of question. But again, I didn't have a lot of options. So, I asked them if I could talk to them for a minute because I had a "very important question." They correctly surmised where this was going by asking if they needed tissues.

We went outside, and I laid it all out, talking about how Karsen is the most amazing person in my life and how it would mean everything to me to have their blessing to ask her to marry me. They were so supportive and said yes right away. They did talk about the challenges we were going to have with my disability and the fact that we're from different faith practices (I'm Catholic and she's a nondenominational Christian). They talked about how if we have children, we will have to work out how we're going to raise them. But they left me with sage advice that if Karsen and I kept Christ at the center of our marriage, they were confident that we'd have a beautiful life together.

With that step complete, it was on to the next project. How exactly was I going to propose?

I came up with an idea with my mom, which required a little deception because, as we had discovered, I couldn't just take Karsen to a special place without her knowing something was up—or worse, not being dressed for the occasion. For instance, I could have asked her to go down to the beach on a random visit there, but she probably would have dressed in beach gear, maybe an oversized sweatshirt and jeans. That's not exactly how she'd want to look for the day she gets engaged so we'd practically have to redo the photos.

I had to convince her I had a speaking event that she'd be driving me to. That way, she would be dressed for the event and not be suspicious of why we were going to a beach resort. My mom helped me scout this out, and I have to say we did some great reconnaissance work.

I told Karsen that I had been booked for a corporate event to be held on February 18, 2023, at the Seascape Beach Resort in Aptos, which is just south of where her parents live. We drove down, and I lucked out because it was a beautiful day. It rained the day before and then the day after. We got sunshine and a relatively warm day as we looked out over the Pacific Ocean. I had also hired a friend of mine who was a photographer to hide out of sight so we could capture the moment.

Karsen started to unload the car as I got out and then I pretended to take a call from the "event planner." Again, I had to fib a little bit here, but I was confident she'd forgive me. I told Karsen that my speech had been delayed by thirty minutes, so we could walk around and take in the view.

It was this amazing spot where we had a view of the ocean in one direction and a view of the bluffs overlooking the water on the other side. This was *the* spot and by this time my nerves were firing. I was amped.

The nerves had started the day before, but I kept them under control. As we walked up, I said I wanted to grab my phone to take a picture. I reached into my bag and pulled out the ring. Karsen was shaking with excitement.

I told her, "I'm sorry, I lied. There is no speech." I poured out my heart and asked her if she would marry me. She said yes. The restaurant manager then walked over with a couple of glasses of champagne, and we toasted to the moment. She was crying and so happy.

As we were driving back to her family's house, I admitted again that I had lied when I told her that we were just going to go have dinner with our parents. Instead, there were about forty-five of our closest friends and family members over at her family's house. It was amazing, and we celebrated all night.

Fortunately, that was the only big planning I had to do. Karsen took over the wedding arrangements, and I was more than happy to get out of the way. Still, when it came down to the planning of our marriage, that was something we were both very intentional about.

We attended an Engaged Encounter retreat, where we

heard talks on everything from finances to parenting to effective communication. We met with other engaged couples and our deacon, and the months leading up to our wedding were filled with incredible energy.

That energy is a by-product of what we have in common. We're both extraordinarily driven, yet we love living away from the hustle and bustle of city life. We love simple time together, such as learning to make a new cocktail or preparing dinner. We also share a wonderful sense of romance.

Like a lot of couples, we had this game that when the clock struck 11:11, we asked each other to make a wish. That's when we kissed for the first time. We were in Berkeley when it was 11:11 and I said I wished that I could get my first kiss from her. Yeah, it's going to make some dudes out there want to vomit, but I'm in love and I'm living the greatest Hallmark movie imaginable.

What wasn't out of a Hallmark movie was my bawling face when Karsen walked down the aisle at our wedding. There wasn't a stoic single tear and a casual dab of the eye. I'm a comically ugly crier. My shoulders shake and my face contorts like Jim Carrey in his prime. The tears flow like water through a broken sprinkler.

I had been holding it all back for the better part of twenty-four hours. The night before I had started to feel the gravity of the moment take me to this place of nervous-yet-happy anxiety. There are moments in life that you savor. They are the ones you forever contemplate as you understand the deeper meaning of the grand scheme of your life. November 11, 2023, was one of those days for me.

Yes, we got married on 11/11 at eleven o'clock. We didn't plan it that way, it just happened.

Waiting at the altar of St. Clare Catholic Church in Roseville, my life changed in a way I once thought would never happen. I married a beautiful, bright, and successful woman from a remarkable family. Karsen could have been with anyone. She could have chosen an easier path with far less risk. Yet, she chose to be with me, and I'm now blessed to share my life with one of the most selfless people ever put on this earth.

Karsen changed how I see my worth and what my future holds. I know I'm loved and, in turn, can give that love back to someone else. The fear I had when I thought, "Who could love this?" has been replaced by hope.

Regardless of what situation you're in, finding people who support you is always worth fighting for. Being loved by one person can be every bit as powerful, if not more powerful, than getting a standing ovation from ten thousand people.

The support I've received isn't just an isolated incident; it's a testament to the universal truth that every person, regardless of circumstance or condition, deserves to feel valued. It reminds us that our worth isn't defined by what we can or cannot do, but by the love we give and receive. I found not only my capacity to care and be cared for, but also the truth that everyone is worthy of love.

REFLECTION QUESTIONS

1. What do you tell yourself about your worth? Are those thoughts shaped by your achievements, or by your inherent value as a person?

2. Think about the people in your life who value you. What do you think they see in you that affirms your worth to them?

3. How can you let the people you love the most in your life know they are valued and loved today?

4. In what ways can you offer more kindness to the people you encounter every day, even in passing?

Chapter 15

TRUE SUCCESS

Staying positive does not mean that things will turn out OK. Rather, it is knowing that you will be OK no matter how things turn out.

—Anonymous

I TOOK AN UNOFFICIAL master's class in my new passion in the fall of 2019.

After speaking to Professor Fulp's class, delivering another speech for Intel, and giving talks to various groups, I realized that motivating others and sharing my story were more than just a hobby. It was a passion I had to dedicate my life to.

At the time, I could give a great twenty-minute speech, but becoming a sought-after subject matter expert in overcoming adversity and captivating large audiences for over an hour was a whole new league. It was time to get serious during my senior year. If you're determined to chase your dream, you seek out someone like Coach Clark and absorb everything he says.

There are very few human beings I know personally who are as dedicated to chasing their passion and mastering their craft as Clark. So, once a week for more than four months during my last year at Cal, Clark and I met to review the elements of my message and the tools I applied to my presentations. We went over every detail, from what I said to how I said it to the visual elements I used.

I'd go over my notes from a previous meeting, write a new draft, and we'd methodically review every word. I'd speak it aloud and then Clark would give a thumbs-up or we would adjust. Depending on his feedback, there might be a rewrite, a visual element to add, or an intonation to change.

Each word was carefully crafted like a painter making strokes on a canvas. I was learning the art of moving hearts and minds. Clark's experience and skill in public speaking, tied with a deep care for me and my success, was the greatest mentorship I could receive as I started this new endeavor. He has a natural sense of how to reach people.

I have some of that too, which led me down this path, and my circumstances have obviously magnified it. I know that when people see me in my wheelchair and hear the story of how I was injured, there is a sense of compassion for me. That's the power of empathy, which is critical for learning and growing from the struggles of others.

It's an important part of what this book reveals, and I hope you find it compelling. But if I'm really going to help people, there has to be more than compassion and a motivating story. As Clark and I were sorting through ideas and practicing my method for delivering them, one central theme kept emerging. Over and over, he emphasized this one point: "Robert, this is about human performance."

Clark made me think about the bigger picture. He made me take time to pause and reflect not just on *what* I've overcome, but *how* I've overcome it. Once I got hurt, my immediate focus was narrowed, centered around surviving and recovering. If I wanted to graduate and accomplish audacious goals, I first needed to breathe on my own.

That was the short-term thinking I needed to survive the initial phase. It took every bit of my focus to get my life back on track.

I was so occupied by the immediacy of my rehabilitation that I hadn't had the opportunity to think about how to fully communicate the principles that drive me. That's an important step because while many find my story inspiring, there are also lots of people who find it unrelatable. Going from a Division I athlete to a quadriplegic and rising out of it is an extraordinary, almost mind-boggling experience. I'm even shocked at times by the things I've been through.

I had to distill years of battling paralysis into key takeaways that anyone could apply to their challenges. Just as I had poured countless hours into my physical rehabilitation, I had to invest that same level of effort into crafting a message that would resonate with anyone facing adversity. The story isn't just about me—it's about unlocking universal truths that lead to success.

My message needed to provide takeaways for big thinkers and dreamers. It had to apply to the person who was growing their career and imagining greatness. I wasn't just helping someone overcome personal challenges; I was also speaking to the corporate leader managing dozens, hundreds, or even thousands of employees.

Whether we're overcoming trauma or striving to reach new heights, the approach to achieving success in these circumstances is interchangeable. Goals are challenges, and challenges are goals. The tools that have helped me battle quadriplegia have helped me graduate from college,

build a thriving speaking career, and help others optimally perform.

These tools are the source of my strength and purpose.
I took Clark's coaching, and it has led to me speaking to
audiences I had only dreamed of when I first started. It
has allowed me to join my passion with my career.

In the six years that I've been speaking, I've had the
opportunity to give well over one hundred keynote presentations to Fortune 500 companies and professional
sports teams and deliver two TEDx talks. I've also shared
my story with students and small businesses looking to be
inspired and informed. Public speaking has allowed me
to connect with thousands of people virtually and travel
across the country to speak in person. It's the meaning of
my life.

I imagine it's the same power any orator feels when captivating an audience. For me, I return to the state of mind
I had before I was injured, when I believed there was a
plan for me. Battling my injury isn't over, but it's far from
holding me back.

The steps I took to get here have proven successful, and
I know they will continue to help me conquer any other
struggles in life.

Much of my life story is unwritten, but these tools will
never change. They are the gift born from the sweat, tears,
and determination of both me and those who have supported me. That's a gift I want to share with you and others.

Control your mindset

Positivity, optimism, and taking on challenges each day
are choices. Regardless of our situation or mood, we have
the power to react in a way that makes us better. When
you feel overwhelmed, simplify your life by making the

decision to keep moving forward. Realize that you can control your mindset, and act on it.

Build a foundation

Don't wait for a challenge to present itself to start strengthening your mind. Work on being your best right now. Do things that make you uncomfortable and use discomfort to strengthen you. Build your foundation now so that when a storm hits, you will stand strong.

Create a vision

Where are you going and why are you doing it? How do you plan to get there? For me, I envision walking again. Am I going to make it a reality? I can never be sure, but having that vision makes me do something every day. It makes me get up and work out. Oftentimes, it's the vision that creates the accomplishment.

Have a mental diet

The key to maintaining a strong frame of mind is the thoughts and ideas you put into your mind. Audit the quality of information you take in, and take deliberate action each day to feed your mind positivity. Just as we feed our bodies to optimally perform, we have to feed our minds to overcome life's challenges.

Keep your sense of humor

When facing a challenge, it's dangerous to be too serious all the time. As difficult as life can be, you have to laugh. You have to maintain some type of joy, even when the restaurant manager doesn't give you a pencil in the Forrest Gump trivia contest.

Make a commitment to others

Giving to others makes the world better, but it helps us too. A selfless mission brings accountability and meaning to life. When we're struggling to find a reason to keep moving forward, our commitment to others is the answer.

Don't delay happiness

Many of us get caught up in the belief that we'll finally achieve happiness when we accomplish a goal. For me, it was about being able to take a step again. I thought that would bring me lasting happiness. Instead, the moment was fleeting, and it taught me the lesson of appreciating what we have right now, not relying on what we hope to have in the future. Goals are important, but life is to be enjoyed.

Compared to what?

It's easy to get caught up in your pain when you are struggling. We can get myopic and forget about the struggles of others. It's imperative to keep perspective and focus on the miracle of what we have and how blessed we are.

Take a stand

We should avoid allowing negative thoughts into our minds, but there comes a point when an injustice becomes too great to ignore. When the pain of knowing our values have been violated outweighs the pain of taking on those uncomfortable emotions and speaking up, we have to stand for what we know is right.

Choose forgiveness

In my case, it would be very simple for me to be swallowed by rage because of how I was injured. The move in that game was illegal and shouldn't have happened. Never receiving an apology only gave me more reason to be angry. But what does rage ever really do for us? Would it somehow provide the healing we need? Obviously not. The decision to forgive is what releases us from being paralyzed by anger and gives us the power to move forward.

Adapt and overcome

Things don't always go as planned. For me, that meant returning to college in a wheelchair. Within that, it's imperative not to let that stop you from moving forward. Use the gifts you still have at the moment. If you do, life may turn out better than you imagined.

Be part of something bigger than yourself

There are standards we must strive to meet if we are to achieve greatness. In my case, that standard was established by men such as Coach Clark, Coach Billups, and many others involved with the Cal Rugby program. Find the group that sets a high standard for you, and let it maximize your potential.

See the gift of challenges

It's not always easy to see, but our greatest challenges are capable of becoming our greatest gifts. My gift is the ability to move people by speaking to their hearts and exposing them to their fears and hopes. Whatever paralyzing situation you're facing, someone can relate. If you can persevere through it, you have the gift to help both yourself and others.

Know you're worthy of love

Nothing important is accomplished alone, and we must seek community to overcome adversity. No matter our circumstances, we all have the capacity within us to give and receive love. Soak up those moments when others lift you up and make it your mission to share that compassion with those around you.

True success

For me, developing these principles has been part of an active way of living. These principles are part of what I believe is the true success of my life.

At the same time, as hard as I've worked these last eight years, and after all of the sweat and tears I've shed to overcome quadriplegia, I haven't achieved the dream ending. Not yet anyway. As the anonymous quote to open this chapter indicates, everything didn't turn out "OK" from a physical standpoint.

The goal I set on May 6, 2017, was to never need a wheelchair again. That hasn't happened. Statistics say that will never happen. Does that mean I've failed? Is all the effort I've put in for nothing?

Absolutely not.

As much as I want to move freely again, it's not the determining factor of success in my life. At the start of my injury, I measured my progress purely by physical outcomes. As I've grown, I've come to find that a victorious life is something far more meaningful.

Success is facing all the challenges this world presents to us while still living with positivity and purpose. We reach the fullness of achievement if our days embody a sense of gratitude and joy. This injury broke my body, but it will never break my spirit, and it will never change who I am.

Since my injury, I graduated from UC Berkeley, I married the love of my life, and I am fulfilling my life's mission to inspire others through the experiences and lessons

I've gained. I accomplished all of this in a wheelchair, but my life is far from paralyzed. This is a life in motion.

What I have found by digging deep into my soul and pouring my heart into serving others is an understanding of how to grow through the circumstances I have been given. I now have a message to share that gives hope and guidance to others as they cultivate their own purpose.

I'm here to show you there is another way to overcome the challenges that may paralyze you. I don't need the ability to walk to understand that my life is a blessing. I have been given a gift that is far more powerful than the ability to go from point A to point B on my feet.

If I didn't get hurt, my life would have had its share of joy and success, but I don't think I would have the meaning that I find now. I wake up every day with something to fight for, and I now have a stronger ability and desire to make a positive impact on the lives of others.

It is something so indescribably special to live with that purpose, especially after being paralyzed.

In the simplest terms, it is powerful.

REFLECTION QUESTIONS

1. If success had nothing to do with achievements or accolades, what internal qualities would define your own success?

2. How can you align those internal qualities of success with your daily decisions and actions?

3. How has this book changed the way you view your challenges or the things that paralyze you?

4. Which tools from this book resonate with you the most? How will you use them to make a difference, not just in your life, but in the lives of others?

www.ingramcontent.com/pod-product-compliance
Lightning Source LLC
Chambersburg PA
CBHW061740120626
46550CB00005B/1844